By Andrea Boroff Eagan

❧

WHY AM I SO MISERABLE
IF THESE ARE THE BEST YEARS OF MY LIFE?

THE NEWBORN MOTHER: *Stages of Her Growth*

The Newborn Mother

STAGES OF HER GROWTH

The Newborn MOTHER

STAGES OF HER GROWTH

Andrea Boroff Eagan

LITTLE, BROWN AND COMPANY
BOSTON · TORONTO

FIRST EDITION

This book was written
by a member of the National Writers Union

Library of Congress Cataloging in Publication Data

Eagan, Andrea Boroff, 1943–
    The newborn mother.

    Includes index.
    1. Motherhood — Psychological aspects.   2. Infants
(Newborn)   I. Title.
HQ759.E16   1985   306.8'743   85-4309
ISBN 0-316-20056-5

BP

DESIGNED BY DEDE CUMMINGS

Published simultaneously in Canada
by Little, Brown & Company (Canada) Limited

PRINTED IN THE UNITED STATES OF AMERICA

For Richard,
and for Molly and Daisy

CONTENTS

The Newborn Mother

STAGES OF HER GROWTH

FOREWORD

HOW DOES A WOMAN become a mother? Giving birth is not enough. The high drama of childbirth — equaled in emotional intensity for the adoptive mother by the saga of getting the baby — only clears the way for the beginning of a complex psychological journey. Mothers can tell us all about it, if we ask them the right questions. The questions are simple: "What are you doing? What are you thinking about? How do you feel?"

While we call a woman a mother as soon as she has a child, it will be some time before she herself begins to *feel* like a mother, or like the mother of this particular child, if it is not her first. In the course of her caring for and caring about her infant in the first weeks and months her feelings about the baby will develop and change. And her feelings about herself, her sense of identity, of who she is in the world will also change. She may come to love the child in the first months, or she may not. But whether or not she does so, she and we and her child will all recognize her as a mother.

A woman first begins to feel like a mother as she develops a profound sense of being completely responsible for her child. I don't claim that this sense of responsibility, which usually persists for as long as the mother lives, is anything but culturally determined. There have been, and still are, societies in which the concept of parental responsibility (or parental guilt) simply does not exist: A child's behavior may be attributed to fate, or to the influence of gods or ancestors. The factors that we consider important — the age at which a child is toilet trained or the severity of discipline — are not thought to matter.

3

We, however, do believe that what happens to a child largely determines its character. And that belief affects and in fact often controls our behavior toward our children and our judgment of ourselves as parents. That belief is enforced and reinforced, over and over, in novels and plays and magazine articles, in psychological and sociological studies that search for the roots of adult behavior (especially *mis*behavior, criminal or neurotic) in family relations and childrearing methods. I too believe that what happens to us, as it acts on the character with which we are born, determines what we become. But I believe, too, that this very *belief*, coupled with the insistence that mother is and must be the single crucial figure of the infant's life, makes mothers what we are in this society: deeply attached and always, always responsible.

In the interest of engendering an extraordinary closeness between a woman and her infant, we create an unusual and difficult situation, one which isolates them together as it inactivates the mother. There are cultures in which babies are carried on their mothers' backs while the mothers go about their normal business; the babies are nursed often and sleep with their mothers at night. In other cultures infants are left alone most of the time, lying in a dark hut except during feedings. And there are many societies in which babies, from the age of five or six months, are cared for by other children. The attachment between mother and infant in these cultures will be different from the one we create.

Our particular kind of attachment and its attendant sense of responsibility do not arise at the moment of birth. Like the rest of human character they develop, rooted in the past, shaped and reshaped by a world of influences as they grow. I am seeking, then, to answer the question, "How does a woman become a mother today in North America?" Then, since "mother" is not all there is to any woman, "Once she has become a mother, how does a woman weave the mother into her adult self, the

4

one which is continuous from the time before the baby was born or even conceived?"

This book has taken a very long time to write. It began, in fact, as a rather different book from the one you read today. It was to be an account of the physical, emotional, and social changes that women experience in the six months after having a baby. Although I was already a mother when I began it, I did not yet understand that becoming a mother is a process, one that no one had at that time delineated.

I began by interviewing mothers. At one point, within a period of about three weeks I interviewed several mothers who all had babies of the same age — between four and five months. I could not help noticing, as I later listened to the tapes of those interviews, that all of those mothers had said almost exactly the same thing. While the significance of this similarity did not strike me all at once, I began to develop a suspicion that something was going on. I also realized, as I continued to interview the mothers of older babies, that that something remained unresolved at six months. And so I continued to interview the mothers until the issues seemed to come to a resting point, if not to a final resolution, at nine months after the baby's birth.

I interviewed, in all, fifty-eight women. This seemed to me not a large number. I have, however, seen studies published in the scientific literature in which fifteen subjects were used, two were dropped from the sample, and conclusions were drawn from the fact that eight of the remaining thirteen did one thing and five did another. My fifty-eight ranged in age from fifteen to forty-three. Most were white; six were black, six were latinas, one was Asian. Most were middle class (broadly defined); two were quite wealthy, and five were definitely poor. About two-thirds were college educated; the rest were not, or not yet. I changed their names and in most cases their occupations (but no other characteristics) to disguise their identities and protect their privacy.

Most of the women were interviewed several times. In some cases I did one interview in late pregnancy, for background and a sense of the woman's expectations, then followed her every couple of months for the full nine months after delivery. Some women were interviewed only once or twice. The interviews were without exception long — often taking up to three hours — and open-ended.

Men are here, too, usually, since this is a book about mothers, in minor roles. The impact of babies on marriage is too often not positive (as indicated by a 1976 Ann Landers survey, in which 70 percent of the respondents said having children was a major obstacle to a happy marriage). I offer no real solution for this problem, but the reader may come away with a better understanding of some of the reasons for the strains that babies place on marriages.

Men are also here as fathers — specifically as fathers who "mother." (Fathering, as Nancy Chodorow has observed, is a different sort of business: "We can talk of a man 'mothering' a child, if he is this child's primary nurturing figure, or is acting in a nurturant manner. But we would never talk about a woman 'fathering' a child.") I found only a handful — five, to be precise — of fathers who spent "as much time with the infant as the average mother" (as I defined my requirement). These five constituted a control group. They were all white, middle class, and in their thirties. I wanted to know whether a man in close contact with an infant would go through the same psychological stages a woman does. My answer — tentative, since the size of the sample is tiny and my investigation a good deal less than thorough — will be found in Chapter 5.

At the same time that I was interviewing mothers, I was reading anything that had to do, however remotely, with my subject. It was when I discovered Margaret Mahler's scheme of infant psychological development (especially her concept of the infant's "hatching" in the fifth month), and began to see its parallel in the development of mothers, that this book began to take its final shape.

I am not a psychologist or a sociologist, but I learned to read in those fields, to understand their terms, to recognize the schools of thought and to determine who was grinding whose axe with an eye toward goring whose ox. Some of it was fascinating; some useful. I learned to distinguish a good study from a sloppy one, a sound theory from sound and fury. In the end, like everyone else, I used what seemed useful, applied what seemed sensible to me.

Writing, as writers are always eager to tell you, is a lonely process, but writing a book like this is, in a curious way, also a collective activity. Here, most obviously, the mothers, and the fathers, who gave me so many hours of their time, whose candor and humor and insight fill this book, were the major contributors.

Writers who write in or near academic disciplines often need the guidance of experts in those fields and often have difficulty finding it. I was most fortunate that Anni Bergman, Judith Kuppersmith, Michael Lewis, and Susie Orbach were all kind enough to listen at length to my problems and my theories in various stages and to give me the benefit of their expert counsel and criticism. Their questions and observations have sharpened and improved my work. Dozens of others gave advice and support and suggested sources and subjects; among them, Madeline Belkin, Vicky Breitbart, Jeanne Fenner, Sandra Fields, Lily-Scott Formato, Joanne Gates, Lois Gould, the late Ellen Moers, Alice Radosh, and Rosalind Ungar stand out.

Madelon Bedell and Nancy Milford provided things without which this book would not have been written. On the basis of I know not what evidence, they showed unflagging confidence in me, in this project, and in my ability to complete it, from its very earliest stages. Their friendship always heartened me, and their confidence fueled my own determination over this very long haul.

The research for this book was done, for the most part, in the incomparable New York Public Library, where I spent several years holed up in the excellent Frederick Lewis Allen Room. The Writers Room was my home for several years more. Without its quiet, its community of writers, and the extraordinary sensitivity to writers' needs of its two directors, Abby Schaefer and Dey Gosse, this book would not exist.

Some of the writing of this book was done at two of those remarkable institutions, the writers' colonies: The Millay Colony and the Ragdale Foundation each provided a month of the wonderful concentration on work that seems only to happen there. P.E.N. and the Author's League Fund both provided support for which I remain truly grateful.

My sisters at HealthRight, especially Barbara Ehrenreich, Naomi Fatt, Sharon Lieberman, Belinda Sifford, Heleena van Raan, and Ginny Reath; and Elayne Archer, Carla Cassler, Abigail Connell, Rachel Fruchter, Ellen McTigue, and Suzanne Williamson have my unfailing affection and warmest thanks. They provided subjects, encouragement, information, and useful skepticism over the life of this project. My gratitude goes as well to my friends and colleagues in the National Writers Union, who sustained and supported me through the last stages, read the manuscript, and gave my life a new direction.

Genevieve Young, a woman of saintly patience and extraordinary editorial skill, is very much responsible for what coherence and clarity the reader will find here. Perdita Burlingame's trenchant comments on the manuscript helped immeasurably to both broaden and sharpen it.

We all have mothers; I am most fortunate in mine, whose support and love has never failed, even when her faith in my completing this book in her lifetime did. There is no possible way to thank her enough. Molly, who the reader will meet in the following pages, is the daughter that every mother should have: good-humored, bright, and talented, with enough of her own ambitions to be tolerant of her mother's. Daisy, too young to be in this book, but born in time to benefit from what I learned in writing it, has brightened all our lives and provided comic relief. My daughters have kept me honest, made me aware of my limitations, and taught me much, some of which is in this book. Richard, my husband, has in the end done the most, by always, always believing in me.

CHAPTER 1

THE FIRST MONTH
The Fog

1

⮑ THE BABY didn't breathe. I could see in the mirror that he was blue and limp. The obstetrician and the intern and a couple of nurses were all over him, yelling at each other and doing things I couldn't make out. I felt very far away on the delivery table, groggy from pain killers and exhaustion and pain. Ed held my hand and kept squeezing it, and neither one of us breathed at all. My other hand was strapped down, and I remember wanting to brush my hair out of my eyes, but I couldn't move and I was too terrified to speak. I just lay there knowing it was all for nothing and the baby was dead.

Ages later (it was really only about two minutes) there was a gagging sound, and I heard a cry and then, finally, I breathed. The nurse picked up the baby and carried him off somewhere, and I heard Ed ask, "Is he all right?" and the doctor said, "Fine, just fine." I felt all the tension go out of me all at once, like a wave washed over me and took everything with it. I heard the doctor say, "OK, let's get the placenta out," and, what seemed from nowhere, this nurse landed on my stomach. I would've screamed, only she had knocked the wind out of me. She was pounding and kneading and squeezing, and I finally got enough breath to say, "Please stop it," but she kept right on, and she said, "Have to get the placenta out, honey. Can't have you getting infected." It was the worst thing that happened all night. I just lay there clutching Ed's hand and crying. After a while, my uterus began to contract again, and the placenta came out. I thought everything was finally all over, and then the doctor said, "Now we just have to sew you up nice and tight." I didn't think I could stand one more thing being done to my body, and the stitching seemed to go on and on.

While he was still sewing, the nurse came back carrying this white bundle. This time, she was very chirpy. She said, "Here he is, dearie, healthy as can be." So she handed me the bundle, and I looked at him and he looked at me, and I swear I didn't feel a thing. Not a thing. I smiled so they wouldn't all think I was abnormal, but I just couldn't have been less interested. I gave him to Ed, and I was relieved when they took him away to the nursery. *All* I wanted was to be left alone. I felt empty and exhausted.

A few hours later, Ellen's energy had returned. She had successfully weathered nineteen hours of labor, a combination of sedative and labor-stimulating drugs, and the certainty, near the end, that she was going to die. But now she was wide awake and euphoric. She sat in bed talking on the telephone, first to her mother, then her sister, her mother-in-law, and one by one, her friends. To each she recounted everything she could remember of her triumph, the delivery of her 8½-pound son. Ed had been down the hall to look at the baby through the nursery window. The baby was sleeping off the effects of the drugs his mother had been given in labor, but he was otherwise healthy.

At six in the evening, twelve hours after the delivery, the baby was at last brought to his mother for feeding. Still drugged, he was hard to rouse, and Ellen was finally beginning to feel the effects of two days and a night without sleep. Though she unwrapped his blanket and took off his diaper to make sure he had all the necessary parts, she felt no great interest. On his part, the baby showed no great interest in being fed, and once again Ellen felt relieved, if guilty, when the nurse came to take him away. An hour later the baby was safely back in the nursery, and Ellen's visitors began to arrive. She was wide awake again, responding to their interest and concern, delighted to be the center of attention.

We have all been assured by the myth of the maternal instinct that a woman will be overcome by feelings of love when she holds her infant in her arms for the first time, but our real lives belie the myths made about them. Love at first sight, whether for a handsome stranger or a newborn baby, is rare indeed. Ellen was thirty when her son Daniel was born. A successful, competent, happily married woman, she passionately desired a child and was pleased to have a son. But her feelings on first seeing him were not what she expected, and she was terribly disappointed. "I was so busy worrying about whether I was still alive that it was hard to get interested in this kid," she explained a few days later, "except that the kid was alive, too."

Heavy, tired, waiting and tired of waiting, a woman at the end of pregnancy is absorbed in herself; whatever claims there may be on her attention, there is a part of her that remains focused on herself and the expected baby. She eats, sleeps, or lies awake trying to sleep. Her pelvic joints have loosened in preparation for the passage of the baby, and in consequence she waddles. She indulges her nesting instinct as well as she can. We do not, in our culture, build birthing huts, but we have our own customs — scrubbing all the floors, painting the baby's room, readying the clothes, practicing the special breathing for labor. The woman about to deliver will also speculate obsessively about the impending event of childbirth. There is little that can shake a woman at this stage from her preoccupation, and the number of things that can distract her dwindles as the days pass. She did not arrive at this state of self-absorption all at once; nor will she emerge from it all at once. The state persists, in fact it intensifies, during labor and delivery and does not end even with the birth of the baby.

In the early stages of labor, a woman is usually quite capable of carrying on a conversation, doing household chores, or reading between contractions. As the labor accelerates, she becomes more focused on the process itself, on the sensation of contractions, the movements of the baby, the stretching of the birth canal. Even if the pain is not overwhelming, she will use the short intervals between contractions to catch her breath and gather her strength. She will not notice noises from the street outside. In the late stages, she will be largely unaware of events in the same room. Birth attendants often find it necessary to shout their instructions to the laboring woman, just to get through to her. As Ellen described it, "I just wanted to be able to concentrate on what was going on in my body, but I kept having to pull myself out of myself to deal with the doctor and the nurses. I always felt like they were interfering."

In the last few minutes of labor, unless someone does interfere, a woman's energy and attention become centered deeply on her body and the violent events taking place within it. Even when a mirror is available so that the woman can watch the birth, a surprising number keep their eyes shut, unwilling to break that intense internal focus. In the very last moment the self-absorption, the concentration is total.

Often overwhelming the woman, too, at this moment, is the fear of death. Just as the self-absorption of the last stage of delivery is an extension of the growing self-involvement of late pregnancy, the terror that seizes many women during delivery seems to be the culmination of the massive anxiety of late pregnancy. T. Berry Brazelton has reported that interviews with a group of pregnant women "in a psychoanalytic interview setting, uncovered anxiety which often seemed to be of pathological proportions." These feelings, "loaded, distorted, so near the surface," he believes are normal and "become a force for reorganization, for readjustment to her important new role." The themes of death and birth are closely linked in psychology and myth, and it may be that the only possible metaphor for the loss of so large a part of oneself as the baby has become is death.

A woman's sense of her physical self is likewise diminished during labor as she sheds any identity save that of laboring woman. Many women have commented, often with surprise, on their lack of physical modesty during childbirth. It is as if, in the late stages of labor, the centering of attention on the inside of the body is so complete that the outside ceases to matter. Disheveled hair, streaming sweat, water, blood, excreta are of no consequence whatever. Concern for appearance, so much a part of the psyche of most women, does not reappear for some time — hours or even days after delivery. The woman's personal boundary has collapsed inward to the womb and reextends itself only gradually. One minute after the baby's birth, or two or five, when she is given it to hold for the first time, the woman's self is not yet large enough to encompass the child. She remains within herself and the infant seems alien.

The act of giving birth, mysterious and most private, is kept so by the woman's capacity for shutting out everything but the essence of the process itself. The need to be undisturbed (though not alone) may explain at least in part the rage and sense of violation that so many women express concerning standard hospital practices. The lights, the noise, the restraints, the orders, the examinations, the air of crisis that exists in even the most routine of hospital births is a brutal intrusion on a woman's need to enwomb herself.

Whether or not a woman who has birthed without undue intrusion will show immediate interest in the baby is a matter of some controversy. Home births, which under the best circumstances involve little more than encouragement and "baby-catching," are often cited as a test of what is normal or natural behavior. In one series of home births reported by midwife Raven Lang, the mothers are all ecstatic and immediately pick up their infants. Everyone present at one of these births seems drawn to look at the baby and shares the mother's euphoria. Brazelton, commenting on those reports, writes:

In many other cultures, the first 30 minutes after birth are devoted to the mother herself. She seems to need and prefer a recovery period of her own before she becomes interested in the infant. . . . I think the ecstasies we see may in larger part be related to her relief at having finally made it to the other end of labor. This euphoria can certainly be mobilized to attach to the infant, and in American culture, where so many roadblocks have been institutionalized, mothers who are experiencing home births may be demonstrating behaviors that are signs of relief at having their autonomy intact.

To some degree, even at a time of very high stress, women will respond to expectations, and this may also be going on in the home births. I have seen home births in which the euphoria is not directed especially toward the baby, and in which the mother seems to respond most positively to attention to herself.

Whatever behavior on the part of the mother might be normal has little opportunity for expression in the modern hospital. The alien atmosphere, the mysterious equipment, and the company of strangers are not conducive to the expression or even the recognition of deep and complex new emotions.

What people do in the first minutes and hours after birth varies from culture to culture. In some, the baby, once it is breathing, is laid aside while attention is turned to the mother. In others, the baby is handed to the mother as soon as the cord is cut. Some cultures practice immediate breastfeeding; others prohibit it for several hours or days, during which time the baby may be nursed by another, fed ground-up or prechewed foods, or not fed at all.

In most hospitals in this country, the baby is whisked to the nursery within minutes of its birth and remains there for up to twenty-four hours, occasionally even longer. More progressive hospitals return babies to their mothers for feeding or for rooming-in after eight to twelve hours. This complete separation of mother and infant seems to be almost unique to our culture:

Even societies that prohibit early feeding of the baby don't isolate it from its mother.

Immediate and prolonged separation of babies and mothers is but one instance of the way one kind of interference in childbirth calls forth another and how each in turn is institutionalized. In this case, the apparent need for separation arose with the routine use of sedatives, anesthesia, and instruments during labor and delivery. All drugs given to the mother during labor eventually cross the placenta and wind up in the baby's bloodstream. A drug which has sedated the mother will, of course, sedate the baby. While the mother's system can clear the drugs in a few hours, the baby's may take several days, sometimes up to a week, to do the same job.

At best, the drugged baby will be sleepy and sluggish. Her temperature may be low, and she may show little interest in her surroundings or in being fed. At worst she will have difficulty breathing. Given a baby in such condition, it is no wonder that the doctors feel the need to keep an eye on her. And until the effects of the drugs wear off, there has seemed little reason not to give both mother and baby a chance to rest and recover. But by now, the separation is simply routine and occurs even when no drugs have been given. Mothers, even those who feel rather detached from their infants, generally hate it. Ellen said: "The day after Daniel was born, I walked down the hall to the nursery to see him, and he was crying. No one was paying any attention to him, and he looked so helpless and angry. I knocked on the door and asked the nurse if I could hold him, and she said no, I wasn't scheduled to get him until the six o'clock feeding. I went back to my room and cried."

Babies are kept from their mothers in these early hours and days, we are told, for their own good; that is, for observation. Often, because of a slightly low body temperature, the baby, even though she is in no way premature, is placed in the additional isolation of an incubator. The "natural" method of keeping the temperature normal and steady — cuddling up to Mom —

is not considered sufficiently reliable, and any observations that a mother might make would be unscientific and therefore useless.

Mothers have always observed their babies, not out of scientific curiosity, but from real interest, and because, when you spend most of your time with someone else, there's little way not to observe their behavior. Thus mothers have long been aware that their infants looked at them and recognized them, listened to them when they spoke, and responded differently to different people. Doctors, on the other hand, believed that babies could neither see nor hear and were certainly incapable of recognizing individuals and differentiating among them. They assured mothers that the mothers were imagining that babies could do all these advanced things. The mothers were right. Science has come lumbering after us at last to prove, among other things, that babies can see and hear at birth.

A baby minutes old can track a hand moving at a distance of about ten inches from her face. She is attracted to the sight of the human face and will gaze at it in preference to anything else. Newborns focus best at a distance of eight to twelve inches, which is, conveniently, about the distance from an adult's face to the baby's eyes when she is cradled in the adult's arms, as most babies are for feeding. The infant will also turn toward the sound of a human voice, especially one that is high pitched. The ability to locate a voice must involve, as it does in adults, the capacity of the brain to distinguish what comes in one ear from what comes in the other and to locate the direction of the incoming sound by the difference in what is heard by each ear.

It has been postulated, primarily by Marshall Klaus and John Kennell, pediatricians at Case Western Reserve University in Cleveland, that human beings have a specific bonding period, akin to those demonstrably present in goats and geese. Baby geese, if they see an ethologist immediately after they are born, imprint onto him instead of their mother and trail around after him, become attached to him, and apparently think that he *is* their mother. A mother goat, if her infant is taken from her for an hour immediately after its birth, thereafter rejects the kid. But if the kid is with her for even five minutes immediately after the birth, it can then be removed for up to two hours and the mother will accept it and nurse it, although there will be "disturbances in nursing patterns."

Babies are alert in their first hour after birth, especially if they haven't been drugged, and pay particular attention to the faces around them. Klaus and Kennell have concluded after studying mothers and infants that mothers (and fathers, too) are particularly receptive to the infant in the hour after birth, and that this hour is in fact the specific bonding period for human beings. Parents, given their naked newborn, soft lighting, and privacy for an hour immediately following the birth, will touch and stroke it, gaze into its eyes and talk to it in high-pitched tones. Klaus and Kennell argue that contact during the first hour enhances the parent-infant relationship, and that the effects of even one hour of contact can be observed months and even years later. (After the first hour or two of alertness, even the undrugged baby gets drowsy and spends most of the next few days sleeping off the effects of being born.) In Klaus and Kennell's study fourteen first-time mothers were given their babies for one hour within the first two hours after birth and for five extra hours (above the usual time allotted for feeding) during each of the next three days. A matched group of fourteen mothers had a more routine experience: "a glimpse of the baby at birth, a brief contact for identification at 6 to 8 hours, and then visits of 20 to 30 minutes for feedings every four hours." The mothers in both groups were questioned and their behavior with their babies was observed at one month, one year, and two years after the birth.

The questions asked at the one-month interview included: "When the baby cries and has been fed and the diapers are dry, what do you do?" A score of zero was given for letting the baby cry, and a score of 3 was given for picking the baby up every time. "An intermediate score was given for behavior falling between these two extremes." The extended-contact mothers scored higher than the control group on the questionnaire, as well as in observations of how close they stood to their babies during an examination by a pediatrician and how much time they spent face to face with the baby during feedings at one month and one year. Klaus and Kennell concluded that the extra hours of contact during the immediate postpartum period made the difference. They believe that early and extended contact, for parents of premature and sick babies as well as for parents of healthy, full-term infants, may reduce the incidence of neglect and abuse that the children may suffer because the attachment of the parents to the child will be so strong as to preclude them.

Numerous questions have been raised about the work of Klaus and Kennell. The population they studied was one of clinic patients, mostly young and poor, many unmarried. While the experimental and control groups were matched at the beginning of the study for sex and weight of the infant and for socioeconomic status of the mothers, no attempt was made to determine whether the groups remained comparable over the life of the study.

A study of twenty-four premature and sick middle-class infants separated at birth from their mothers for treatment, found no difference at one year between these infants and a similar group of babies not separated from their mothers, using the customary measures of attachment (which are not above criticism themselves). The authors of this study held that "attachment patterns are influenced by maternal-infant interaction over a period of time and provide evidence for the resiliency of infants in their formation of attachment patterns." Certainly adoptive parents, parents of premature babies who spend weeks or months in hospitals, and parents whose babies are subjected to routine separation in hospitals can form close, strong, and lasting bonds with their infants.

Klaus and Kennell's insistence on the particular responsiveness of mothers (I am deliberately excluding fathers here) to their infants in the hour after birth is especially peculiar because of the frequent reports from mothers of being *un*interested in the baby just after it is born.

In Klaus and Kennell's experiment, we have to assume that the extra hour of contact with the baby was announced to the mothers with an air of its being something special, which it in fact was in that hospital. It is just possible that a nurse's cheery "Now we're going to let you hold your baby for an hour," would signal to a young, inexperienced mother that something was expected of her, as indeed it was. And judging the mothers' behavior by their response to their babies' crying seems particularly unfair, since these women might not have known that current opinion among psychologists holds that it is good to pick up the baby when it cries, and that the baby won't become demanding, spoiled, and bad-tempered, as the experts used to insist it would.

Whatever the flaws in bonding research, few parents would argue against the opportunity to have their babies with them as much as possible. No one who has given birth at home or in a birthing center is unaware of the peaceful quality of the hours after the baby is born when there is no threat that the baby will be taken away. The parents are free to hold the baby and gaze at it, to bathe or feed it, or to let someone else take care of it. Some mothers, free to do whatever they want, desire only to be with the baby, to hold it, and to talk to it as the mothers in the bonding experiments do. Other mothers are content to allow themselves to be washed, to change their clothing, to eat and drink a celebratory glass of champagne while someone else cleans and cuddles the baby. The mother, confident that she can have the baby whenever she wants it, doesn't feel that she must take advantage of a special and limited opportunity granted by hospital authorities.

William Ray Arney believes that the bonding research has gained currency because the medical establishment needs a scientific reason for changing long-standing practices like that of separating mothers and babies. That enforced separation, of course, is just one of the procedures that is driving women away from the hospital when it comes to choosing where to have the baby. "Early separation of mother and infant and little contact after birth developed," Arney writes, "out of 'scientific' concern over the introduction of infectious diseases into the newborn nursery. . . . Practices that have their own scientific basis cannot simply be changed in a profession the very existence of which is dependent on the authority that science, or at least a facade of scientism, affords it." Arney believes that Klaus and Kennell's research made a change in hospital policy permissible, while women's complaints and flight from hospitals and obstetricians made it necessary. We therefore find ourselves championing the conclusions of this unscientific science, because, in fact, it only makes sense. It does, after all, seem logical that two people will form a stronger attachment if they are together than they will if they are separated, especially if they have barely met and one of them can't talk.

As we will see in Chapter 2, a long and complete separation, especially when there is doubt about the baby's survival, may interfere with a mother's feelings for her infant. In preliterate societies, where many babies do not survive, there is perhaps some logic to keeping a distance between the mother and baby at first, laying the baby aside for an hour or so while the mother is tended to or prohibiting breastfeeding for up to three days. A baby born in very poor health can be allowed to die, and its mother, never having held it or really seen it, may be protected from overwhelming grief. Infanticide, where it is practiced, is most often committed at the moment of birth — so that the infant never takes its first breath — or within the first few hours, before the mother is attached to it and before the baby is granted social status as a human being.

In a society like ours, where the vast majority of infants survive and where the attachment of at least one caretaker to the infant is crucial (since there is no community that will take over from inadequate parents), anything that enhances attachment, even in the short term, needs to be encouraged. "It is not that mothers cannot attach after such separation," writes Brazelton, "it is that it may be more expensive — and unnecessarily so. And in stressed situations, where there is little or no reason to want a baby or to want to attach to him, the difference may be critical." For Ellen and Daniel, the separation was not a disaster, but it certainly added a negative element to an already complex emotional situation.

Despite their considerable abilities, newborn infants are somewhat limited as a topic for discussion. After all, once you have told someone the baby's sex and weight and described the color of her eyes and hair, if she has any, there isn't much more to say. Women in the hospital do not spend much time discussing their babies. They talk among themselves about themselves. A mirror of the days of self-involvement, anxiety, and fantasy preceding the birth, the days after are spent retelling what happened.

The need to recount the labor and delivery is akin to the need to tell the story of any major life event. Running a marathon, surviving an accident, graduating with honors all gain reality from retelling. Talking about childbirth helps to make it real, to convince the woman that it actually happened, and at the same time to distance her a little from the more unpleasant aspects of the experience. There is often a gradual distortion of the event, which can begin as early as a few hours afterward. For some, the distortion involves an exaggeration of the difficulty of the delivery, so that the woman can feel she has truly triumphed. For others the pain and fear and the anger at doctors and nurses are rapidly deemphasized, and the experience acquires an increasingly rosy glow.

These distortions have obvious psychological benefits. Ellen, whose delivery was described at the beginning of this chapter, told me when I first spoke with her a few hours after the birth that Daniel "came out screaming." It was several weeks later, after she had seen a film made of the birth, that she gave me an accurate description of what had happened. The speed with which she had misremembered the actual events of the birth, and the completeness with which she did so, served a purpose. Daniel's imagined entry into the world, screaming, signified for Ellen that he was robust and vigorous, and that she, a first-time mother, did not need to be concerned about his survival or too cautious in her handling. Had she accurately remembered the delay in getting him to breathe, her confidence in her ability to care for him, which was not high to begin with, might have been further undermined.

The newborn infant's personality is, of course, still rudimentary. She may be placid or irritable, eager or wary, sleepy or hungry or curious, but her way of expressing any of these in the beginning is limited. She may feel omnipotent or helpless or both at different times; we cannot really know. But it is easy to imagine that as she emerges from the somnolence of the first two or three days of life, shapes and objects must seem to swim in and out of her field of vision with little cause or reason. While she may think she is the center of all activity, it seems to us that there is not much self at her center. She still exists primarily in a world of physical sensation — warmth and cold, hunger and satiety, startling noises and soothing sounds, the rhythm of her mother's heart that she remembers from her time in the womb, or its absence.

A mother, too, at this time, is concerned with physical sensations: the tightening of her womb and the filling of her breasts, the persistent pain of stitches or nipples, the overwhelming fatigue of a succession of nights with only interrupted sleep, the startle at the unfamiliar sound of the baby's cry, as the newborn startles at a sudden noise.

There are many women who feel at this stage that they are still pregnant, that the baby is still, literally, a part of themselves. "Even the second day after he was born," Ellen said, "I kept waiting to feel him moving inside me. I still felt pregnant, and so I felt very little connection to the baby. He scared me; there seemed to be something unreal about him."

2

However attachment is defined and wherever lie its roots, it has to begin at some point. That point does not often occur in the moments after birth, or even within the first few days. In those first days the mother, and particularly the first-time mother, is still too interested in herself and her experience of childbirth to be able to work up a sustained involvement with the baby. Most women find that the hospital is not a restful environment, and the time with the baby is rarely relaxed and uninterrupted, nor does it usually occur during the infant's rare and brief periods of alertness.

When my first daughter, Molly, was born, the hospital pediatrician ordered her fed on a three-hour schedule because of her small size. Her first feeding was completely successful, but the three-hour schedule was so out of phase with the rest of the hospital's routine, to say nothing of Molly's own cycles of hunger and sleep, that nursing her became increasingly difficult over the next two days. Feedings invariably occurred in the middle of visiting hours, during meals, or when the obstetrician or pediatrician was in the room talking to me. I always felt rushed, and at least half the time Molly was more interested in sleeping than in eating. Feeding time was simply a chore. The night before we left the hospital, in the middle of the night, at my insistence, she was brought to me when she awoke. Finally, it was quiet. No one was bringing a tray, an ice pack, or a pill. The phone didn't ring. The nursery nurse looked in a couple of times, but we were otherwise undisturbed. There was only the soft light of a bedside lamp. Molly opened her eyes and looked right at me. I was completely unprepared for the feeling that overwhelmed me. I understood for the first time that she was mine, my child, and I loved her without question and far beyond anything I had ever imagined. I told her her name, explaining where she was, who I was, and where she had come from.

Several women told me of similar experiences. Rachel, a 27-year-old teacher, came home from the hospital when her son Matthew, her first baby, was three days old. While she liked holding him while they were in the hospital and was pleased that she recognized him when he was brought to her several hours after he was born, she had no strong feelings about him. But on their second day home, when Matthew was four days old, she had a different experience:

ᵔ It was one of those times when I was feeling scared and sad and very, very lonely. I looked down and I saw this tiny little person, and that was all projected onto him, this totally alone little person who didn't know anybody in the whole world, and here he was in this house with strangers. It was suddenly feeling that I had the power to make him feel better that brought on the love for him, but it happened when he was mine, and the hospital wasn't taking him away from me.

These events often happen shortly after the return home, when the mother is at last alone with the baby. The twenty or thirty minutes allotted for feedings in the hospital, and the surrounding commotion, don't seem to be conducive to this kind of development. Two people beginning a love affair would hardly choose thirty minutes in a hospital room as the ideal setting for getting to know each other. Even women who had rooming-in arrangements, and thus had their babies with them all or most of the time, often did not begin to love their babies until they got them home and began to feel responsible for them.

It is usually only with first babies that attachment begins in such a memorable way. The mothers of second or later babies generally described the process as "more gradual." Perhaps because a mother's attention is never focused quite as exclusively on a second baby, simply because of the presence of an older child, incidents like these rarely occur. Women who had home or other out-of-hospital births, including births of first babies, could remember no special moment of attachment, no sudden rush of love. Here it may be that the sense of responsibility for the infant, as well as the feelings of love for it, develop more steadily with uninterrupted contact and virtually no outside interference.

A mother who is with her baby constantly and who has to respond only to her own and the baby's needs, and not to a hospital's schedule, may be sooner aware of her baby's responses to her. Most women who deliver in hospitals have some medication; most women who deliver outside hospitals don't. Thus babies born in hospitals are more likely to show the effects of maternal medication during labor and to be sluggish, sleepy, and unresponsive for a few days. Babies born outside the hospital, with no medication and fewer shocks (less noise, less light, and less being slapped around) are somewhat more alert and responsive. If a mother's feelings of love for her baby depend on the baby's ability to respond to her and her ability to perceive that response, then the delay in feeling attached and its sudden onset may be explained by the need for both to be together, relaxed and uninterrupted, *after* the drugs have worn off. It is only then that there is an opportunity for love.

The second-time mother may be less surprised by the response, since, at least unconsciously, she expects it, and the home-birth mother may simply get used to it gradually. There seemed to be no difference in degree between those whose love arrived all at once and those upon whom it crept up.

The women who were suddenly overtaken by feelings of love and protectiveness for their infants remembered the incident as the high point of the baby's first days. Sometimes the attachment takes much longer to be established — weeks or even months into the baby's life — but it almost always, given a normal baby and a willing mother, happens eventually.

When caring for the baby is very difficult for any reason, attachment is often delayed; and when attachment is delayed for any reason, caregiving can become a burden. Klaus and Kennell argue, and in this most pediatricians and psychologists seem to agree, that "an essential principal of attachment is that parents must receive some response or signal, such as body or eye movements from their infants, to form a close bond. . . . We have abbreviated this principle to: 'You cannot fall in love with a dishrag.' "

It is also very difficult to care endlessly for a dishrag — to feed it, soothe it, and change its dirty diapers ten times a day. One woman quoted by Robson and Moss found all her positive feelings for her baby fading as the baby failed to stop crying when she held him and didn't smile or make eye contact with her. She felt, she said, "estranged and unloved." The baby was later discovered to be brain damaged. Even a normal infant is a chore in this period. If an incident of attachment can be the high point of the first week, an attack of the "third-day blues" (which can occur any time during the first two weeks) can certainly be the low. On Rachel's first day home (the day before she fell in love with her infant son):

✎ I felt very disoriented. Everything just seemed weird. The house looked weird. I started tidying constantly, because if one thing was out of place it just threw me. I had a frantic need to keep control over my environment. John came home, and the baby was crying, and I was crying.

For Ellen, a trivial incident triggered a similar reaction:

✎ The day we came home from the hospital, Ed took the baby into the den, where he was going to watch a football game. I sat down and cried. It was like he was taking my child already.

A chance word, a sentimental TV movie, or simply the sight of the baby can bring on tears. There are many explanations for the third-day blues (sometimes inaccurately called *postpartum depression*, a term also used to describe the more serious, persistent condition that attacks one woman in 1500 in the weeks or months following the baby's birth). The levels of several hormones, particularly estrogen and progesterone, which are very high during pregnancy, drop sharply in the few days before and after delivery. Also, unless hormones have been given to prevent it (and sometimes even if they have), the mother's milk comes in for the first time around the third day, replacing the yellowish colostrum. The breasts at this point may become swollen, hot, and painful, "like hot rocks," as one woman put it. These physiological changes probably account for some of the irritability and weepiness that many women experience. (They are much like certain of the symptoms that some women experience premenstrually, which may also result from changes in hormone levels.)

Not all women experience the third-day blues, however, even though all undergo the physiological changes. In some United States hospitals, the incidence of transient depression has been found to be as high as 80 percent. Klaus and Kennell report their observations of a maternity clinic in Denmark where mothers were not separated from their babies and were encouraged to care for them from birth. There they found postpartum blues were rare. Klaus and Kennell feel that the extended contact of the mothers with their babies and the encouragement they got in caring for them helped to prevent the symptoms. Brazelton, however, commented that the reactions seen in Denmark may reflect "the cultural expectations for not showing one's feelings."

Proponents of home birth claim that there is much lower incidence of postpartum blues among women who give birth at home. Their argument is broader than that of Klaus and Kennell, who attribute the symptoms only to the separation of mother

28

and baby. Home-birth advocates argue that the loss of autonomy and control in hospitals, the use of drugs and instruments, enforced schedules and isolation, as well as separation from the baby, all play a part.

The women I interviewed who had home births did not have third-day blues. Several used the same words — "very smooth" — to describe the course of the first few weeks. These women, it should be remembered, suffered fewer of the incidental discomforts of childbirth than did the women who delivered in hospitals. They had no anesthesia or drugs of any kind. They had no episiotomies, hence no stitches. They nursed their babies on demand, and thus underwent no breast engorgement. They faced no criticism from professionals concerning their handling of their babies. They ate what they wanted, when they were hungry, in familiar surroundings, and when they were able to sleep, did so without being wakened for meals or medication.

Whenever a woman told me that she had had an attack of third-day blues, I asked what she had been feeling at the time. Some said they had no idea what they were crying about, which seems to support a physiological explanation. Others, however, spoke of physical discomfort, of difficulty in establishing breastfeeding, of fatigue, unaccustomed responsibility, and a sense of being not quite fitted for the tasks of motherhood, a sense which was sometimes exacerbated by the critical attitudes of hospital personnel and sometimes even of family members. The discontinuity of the hospital-to-home transition sometimes seems to be implicated as well. Ellen, for one, had a hard time the first few weeks:

> ✍ I liked being taken care of in the hospital. I could be a prima donna. The focus was still on me. I liked that. In the hospital, after he was fed, if he cried the nurse came and took him away, and though I felt guilty about that, I was glad anyway. When he cries at home, nobody takes him away, and I don't know what to do. My insides panic and I feel like he's going to die.

3

Once women are home, they are seldom taken care of. In the United States today the average hospital stay for a woman who has an uncomplicated delivery is three days, and the stay is often even shorter. In the first decades of this century, when most babies were still born at home, the new mother was advised: "The mother, no matter how well she may feel, needs a certain time of rest before she is capable of taking up her ordinary occupations and pleasures, which, if indulged in too early, may result in retarding or stopping altogether the natural restorative processes. Most women are able to sit up in a chair for an hour on the tenth day; they may be walking around the room usually after two weeks and by the end of the month be able to go up and down stairs, but in all cases it is well for the mother to refrain from full activity for six weeks." Even forty years ago it was customary for a woman to remain in the hospital for two weeks or more, confined to her bed for most of her stay, and following her return home to spend most of the next month getting plenty of rest.

So much inactivity requires a good deal of practical support. The management of the household, as well as the daily routines of cooking, cleaning, laundry, and baby care, would require the services of at least one other woman. Help was often provided by the extended family — the mother's mother or mother-in-law, her sisters or daughters. There is an assumption in all the books and pamphlets written for new mothers, until recently, that hired help would be available, as in fact it was to the middle class, and some attention is usually devoted in these books to the matter of choosing suitable servants. In tightly knit communities, even among the very poor, help was provided during the lying-in period. Describing the lives of farm women in the South during the Depression, Margaret Jarman Hagood writes:

There must be an arrangement for someone to take over the housekeeping and cooking duties for a week or so after the child is born while the mother is in bed. This function designated as "staying with" is not to be confused with "grannying" which means assisting during the actual birth process, although sometimes the same person may do both. In a few cases the families could afford to hire someone, usually a Negro woman. The customary practice, however, is for some female relative — mother, sister, niece, mother-in-law, sister-in-law, or cousin — to come and take charge of the housework and of the care of the children for a week or two, for no pay. It is more often done by an older woman whose children are grown, by the family spinster, or by a fairly young woman not yet married. Practicing mothers cannot leave their families for so long a time. Thus this usually unpaid service is not on an exchange basis, but is something that those without children can and are expected to do for the childbearers.

For these poor women, as well as for women who worked outside their homes and those who could neither commandeer nor hire help, the lying-in period must have been much shorter and more active than the six weeks of the middle class. In a dingy tenement walkup or on an isolated farm the housework, cooking, laundry, and child care, in the absence of running water, washing machines, convenience foods, and disposable diapers, were immensely arduous. Where the woman made a financial contribution to the family, whether on the farm or in a mill or shop, she could usually not be spared for long. A diary account from a nineteenth-century frontier farm may describe an extreme case, but it is probably not entirely atypical:

August 6, 1876, was a very warm day and this was the day the threshers arrived at the Stoner farm. Early that morning, grandmother surprised the family by giving birth to a baby boy. . . . This baby was grandmother's tenth child.

She was forty-five years old and this was her last baby. . . . But the men had to be fed and grandmother sat up in bed and peeled potatoes for the crew.

Since World War II, when it was discovered that women in lying-in hospitals in London did not suffer from walking from their beds to bomb shelters during air raids, the prescriptions for bed rest and the length of stay in the hospital have steadily decreased. From the 1940s through the 1960s women in labor were heavily drugged and the babies usually delivered with forceps. The interest in natural childbirth (which began in this country with the publication in 1952 of Grantly Dick-Read's *Childbirth Without Fear*), the gradual recognition of the dangers of medication during labor, and the trend to early walking and early discharge from the hospital after childbirth have combined to create, in some circles at least, a view that childbirth is a normal process, not an illness capped by a medical-surgical crisis. Women's desire to experience childbirth, to be present at the birth of their own babies, has had its influence. But as we have come to understand that childbirth is a normal event, we have rejected the notion that prolonged rest is necessary afterwards.

Economic considerations have supported the new trends. A long hospital stay is prohibitively expensive and often unpleasant as well. The cost of household help is beyond the reach of most families, and the large house that might accommodate a mother or an aunt for an extended stay is more and more a rarity. Few jobs offer adequate maternity leave, making it necessary for many women to return to work within a few weeks. And many women simply feel guilty about lying in bed and letting someone else, anyone else, wait on them. Six weeks of even partial inactivity comes to seem, from whatever angle, an absurdity.

The Biblical period of "uncleanness" after childbirth lasted for six weeks. Numerous preliterate societies grant a new mother six weeks' respite from her everyday responsibilities, even if she is permitted to socialize with the community sooner.

Six weeks is the time usually required for the uterus to return to its prepregnant size and is usually considered by doctors to mark the end of the period of convalescence. Today, however, only a very few women, even if they plan not to return to their jobs for several months, allow themselves to rest for six weeks. There seems to be an element of competitiveness in women's eagerness to get back to normal. The woman who argues a landmark legal case or defends her dissertation or paints her entire house a few days after having a baby is pointed to as a standard to which all women should aspire. We all seem to be trying to emulate the apocryphal Chinese peasant who plowed to the end of the row, lay down in the field to give birth un-assisted, and then resumed plowing. We can only assume that any woman who behaved in such a way did so only from the most compelling economic necessity, aged early, and died young. Ellen stated the modern case succinctly when she commented, "By the third day, I was feeling that I should be back as a functioning adult."

Forty years ago, when six weeks of postpartum rest was the goal, if not the norm, help for the new mother was much more available than it is today. Baby nurses were inexpensive and customarily came to stay for from four to six weeks; families were not yet so widely dispersed. Today, two weeks' help is considered a luxury. Those who can get it, however, do seem to take advantage of it. One woman, who with her husband shared a house with another couple, had her mother come for two weeks after she had her first baby. Her husband stayed home for the first ten days, and the other couple, who also had a child, were available to help out with the baby. The new mother "slept for the whole two weeks."

Elaine, whose husband ran his consulting business from their home and whose parents, in-laws, and grandparents all lived in the neighborhood, told me: "I stayed in bed for the entire first

33

week at home, and for the next month I only got up when I felt like it."

Many women think, or hope, that they'll be able to manage without help, but those who do so successfully are rare. Rachel was more typical:

> ~ John's mother kept saying I had to have a nurse. Everybody kept asking wasn't I going to get somebody. The last thing I wanted was some strange lady in the house. John was wonderfully helpful, but I got anxious about him doing all this work, because he was as tired as I was, since the baby was crying all the time. Now I think I *would* like to have somebody I would pay, whose emotional life I didn't have to worry about. I mean, John didn't want me to worry about him, but it got into sort of a cycle where I was worrying about him worrying about me and he was worrying about me worrying about him, and I couldn't take a nap because I could see he was about to collapse, although he was carrying on valiantly. When he finally went back to work, it was a certain kind of relief. The whole first week back was the baby crying all the time, me having such sore nipples that it hurt to have anything on and not feeling well, but not knowing that I didn't feel well. I never rested. I never took a nap. Partly because I never rested, I'd be a wreck when John got home.

By the end of the first two or three weeks, the immediate aftereffects of the delivery have begun to fade. The recovery proceeds and the recollection of the birth becomes increasingly distorted. In our culture there is usually some help available to the mother for the first two weeks, if only that of a husband who takes some time off from work. But though the mother has only just begun to get over the pregnancy and the delivery and to become sometimes painfully aware of the demands of the infant, after two weeks the help is withdrawn and most women are on their own.

Being alone is often a relief at first, as it was for Rachel. The new mother trusts or hopes that things will now somehow return to normal. While help is usually welcome in the beginning, most people's lives do not easily permit another resident in the home and most houses do not easily accommodate long-term guests. Baby nurses are notorious, as are some grandmothers, for monopolizing the baby, believing that their expertise is better for the newborn than the mother's clumsy attempts at caregiving. However, especially if the baby is the mother's first, they may leave behind a woman who hasn't the least idea of how to change a diaper, much less give the infant a bath. These simple skills are, of course, quickly learned, and it is more than unusual to hear of a baby inadvertently drowned in the bath. It appears that we assume that a woman, after two weeks, will be able to resume her usual activities, as well as full care of the baby, without further help from others. If she doesn't, she may find herself accused, or feel herself accused, of malingering. Many women sounded apologetic about how they were managing, a scant two weeks after giving birth. One mother said:

✌︎ Even though I'd been taking most care of the baby, after my mother left I felt absolutely helpless. If I took care of the baby, I couldn't do anything else. I thought he'd sleep and I could get the housework done, but some days my husband would come home from work, and I'd still be in my robe, and the coffee cups from breakfast would still be in the sink. I got horribly depressed.

Rachel, referring to the second two weeks of the baby's life, made this comment:

✌︎ I kept reading in the books, "The baby is more important than the housework," and I suppose they say that to be comforting to you: "Don't worry if the house is a mess." I felt worse if the house was a mess. I couldn't *stand* it. So if I tidied and he was crying, then of course I was doing something terrible to him.

Anne, who had a three-week-old daughter and a three-year-old son, said:

> ~ The first two weeks at home I had the feeling I'd done something tremendously important. Then it seemed like my act of having delivered a baby didn't matter any more, and I started getting very, very depressed. It was like everyone had gone on and forgotten about me.

Women who lived in extended families or communes, who had relatives nearby, or had money enough to hire help, fared reasonably well. For the others, the third week of the baby's life began the first of several difficult periods. The new mother's insecurity at this point can be exacerbated by professional and nonprofessional advice. Pediatricians and child-care manuals now agree, for the most part, that air is not harmful to little babies, and that infants can be taken outdoors without ill effect soon after they are born. There is still disagreement, though, on just how much fresh air is actually safe, and even Dr. Spock sounds ambivalent:

> It would be good for every baby weighing 10 pounds or more to be outdoors, when it isn't raining, for 2 or 3 hours a day, as long as the temperature is above freezing and the wind isn't bitterly cold. An 8-pounder can certainly go out when it's 60° or above. . . .

It seems a bit complicated, and there's no telling what you should do if your baby weighed 6 pounds, 12 ounces, or, like mine, didn't weigh 10 pounds until she was five months old. The new mother, in an effort to appear conscientious, or at least not reckless, so as not to incur the disapproval of her possibly less enlightened neighbors, may keep her infant and herself indoors for weeks on end, away from cold or damp or heat or dust or criticism or companionship.

Also increasing the new mother's burden is fear of infection. Many primitive societies keep mother and infant in relative isolation for about two weeks, reducing the risk of infection for both, but by the end of two weeks the infant, if healthy, is generally considered to be sufficiently robust to be exposed to its friends and neighbors. Though medical opinion is more lenient than it was a few years back, the fear of communicable disease is still pervasive enough for many mothers to wonder whether it is safe to have strangers, and particularly children, near the infant. The breastfed baby acquires immunities through her mother's milk, and even the formula-fed infant is not so vulnerable that she needs to be isolated. To protect the child, fear of illness, like fear of cold air, causes many a mother to stay inside with her baby at a time when support and companionship are becoming necessary.

John D. Benjamin, who has done electroencephalographic studies of infants, found that between the third and fourth weeks of life there is what he calls a "maturational crisis." (It should be kept in mind that his data are collected on full-term infants, or are corrected for full term. If a baby in his study was born two weeks before her due date, she would reach the stage in question about two weeks later than the baby born at term, in this case at five to six weeks of age.) Benjamin reports:

> As compared with neonates, babies at this age (3–4 weeks) show a marked increase in overall sensitivity to external stimulation. . . . Without intervention of a mother figure for help in tension reduction, the infant tends to become overwhelmed with stimuli, with increased crying and other motor manifestations of undifferentiated negative affect.

The problem for the mother is that in our culture there is no mother *figure* for help in tension reduction. There is only mother herself.

Another researcher, Richard Q. Bell, remarks of this stage: "In the first month or so, there is a period during which the mother is in essence at the mercy of the crying of her infant." A woman who is suffering the exhaustion brought on by several weeks without a full night's sleep, who may still be feeling the discomfort of stitches or sore nipples or hemorrhoids, is required to resume all her normal activities at nearly the same moment that her infant becomes "overwhelmed with stimuli, with increased crying. . . ." A new mother, at this point, can easily begin to feel inadequate. Even though the baby has measurable responses to her mother, these reactions are subtle and easily missed and don't afford the mother much reward. In fact, the second half of the first month, when the newness of the newborn has worn off just a bit, is the time when the complaint, "She doesn't *do* anything," is most frequently heard from parents.

None of the women I interviewed, not even those who had fallen in love with their babies in the beginning, and none of the 54 mothers studied by Robson and Moss in their research on attachment, felt attached to the babies at this stage. By two weeks of age it can be shown experimentally that a baby can recognize her mother's face, voice, and smell. The net effect of this remarkable skill, however, may be an increased strain on the mother. If the baby quiets for anyone, it is most likely to be for her mother, making the mother the irreplaceable tension reducer for a difficult and irritable infant, one for whom she has little positive feeling. As Ellen described it:

> ~ Coming home, you're still elated, you still have all those juices going. Whoever you're living with is still spending time at home. The baby is still an object of curiosity. But after all that excitement of people and presents, suddenly the baby is not sleeping all the hours they do when they're very tiny. That's the worst time. One night the baby was crying and crying, and I was sitting with him and rocking, and the pat-pat-patting suddenly turned into a karate chop. I burst into tears, too, then.

Brazelton believes that feelings of depression are universal in these early weeks. From my interviews, however, it appears that women who have enough help do not become depressed, although no one claimed to find the early weeks especially rewarding. It is the combination of unrewarded work, fatigue, and isolation that are devastating. Anne, with a three-week-old and a preschooler, had a typical reaction when her expected relief did not arrive on time one night:

> ✌︎ One day last week, Vince came in an hour and a half late and didn't apologize. I was absolutely furious. I had this excessive rage that I couldn't stop, and what made it worse was his not understanding what it was all about. He got home and the dinner wasn't made, and I just sat there rocking the baby. I hadn't *managed*, and he was angry at me for not managing. And there was a part of me that wanted to manage, and I felt guilty and drained and I kept thinking: "What's wrong with me? Why can't I manage better?"

The assumption made by many investigators that postpartum depression (of either the transient or the long-term type) is the result of a woman's rejection of the mothering role does not stand up well to scrutiny. All women experience anxiety during pregnancy and the early weeks of the baby's life. Even when the mother has developed a strong and early feeling of love for the baby, in most cases it does not last, simply because the baby does not reciprocate in any recognizable way. So, like a crush on a person who does not respond, the feeling fades and passes, smothered in this case by growing exhaustion and a dawning feeling of entrapment and unending responsibility.

For the woman who expects to love her baby unreservedly from the time it is born, and who depends on the appearance of maternal instinct to allay her sense of incompetence, these early weeks are particularly distressing. Even for a woman who makes no unreasonable demands on herself (though such a woman is hard to imagine, given the expectations that most of us seem to have of ourselves), the early weeks offer little satisfaction or reward. But it is the woman whose high expectations

39

conflict with bleak reality who is most likely to become severely depressed. Placing an excessively high value on her capabilities as a mother and on her ability to love her infant predisposes her to disappointment. It is, in fact, the woman who accepts the traditional mothering role most completely who is at highest risk.

Postpartum depression as Brazelton defines it — feelings of exhaustion, anxiety, and inability to cope with new demands and responsibilities — may be nearly universal, but it is not inevitable. One study found significantly fewer postpartum emotional problems in a group of women who were informed about what to expect in the early weeks and advised to establish a support network of family and friends in advance of the birth, compared to a control group. Common sense alone, of course, should tell us that a woman who knows what to expect from a new baby, who gets encouragement and practical help and a chance to rest every day, would weather the early weeks better than a woman without those advantages.

The women I interviewed, even those who could have left their babies with their own mothers or sisters, or with close and trusted friends, were reluctant to leave the babies with anyone else during the early weeks. "I just couldn't imagine doing that," was Rachel's typical reaction. There were those who did leave the babies — to go out to dinner with their husbands or, in a couple of cases, out of the necessity of an early return to a job — but it wasn't easy.

There is no mention in the literature of mothers' reluctance to leave their infants in the first few weeks, and none of the mothers had a good explanation for her unwillingness to be separated from the baby. "It's not like I'm so crazy about him that I can't bear to be parted from him for an hour, but I just can't leave him with someone and go," Ellen said. A mother may recognize that her own tie to the baby is weak, and the insecurity arising from the weakness of that tie may be projected onto anyone else who might care for the baby. If you cannot trust your own feelings for your child, how can you trust those of someone else? It is also possible that the baby's obvious vulnerability triggers a protective response in its mother, making her reluctant to part from it.

The disinclination to leave the baby or to take it out of the house, along with exhaustion and the decline in the number of other adults in the house, whether helpers or visitors, can combine in the second half of the first month to produce a degree of isolation that is unusual for an adult in our society. Many of the women also seemed to have an active aversion to the outside. When I asked Ellen at the end of the first month if she had been out of the house, she replied, "Only twice. I don't like it out there." Whether these women keep to their houses by choice or by circumstance, they wind up spending most of their time alone, in the house, with the baby. The baby is not the only one at this stage who feels suddenly assaulted by stimuli. The mother does too, and isolating herself in her house is one way to minimize the number of things she has to contend with. She tries to limit herself to essentials, but sometimes even the essential is too much.

Most of what the baby does at this point in its life is dictated by internal drives. Hunger, fatigue, and irritability all arise from within to determine the baby's behavior. Even its little fleeting smiles appear, not in response to its mother's presence or voice or smile, but from the satisfaction of a full stomach or a change of position, or some other reduction of stress. While the mother may be — probably is — responsible for the reduction of stress, the baby's smile is too indirect to be much reward. The baby seems turned in on itself, concerned with its internal processes.

The psychologist Margaret Mahler has called this the stage of "infantile autism," and the metaphor is appropriate to describe a being concerned almost entirely with what is going on inside itself. The mother, too, could be described, if one wanted to stretch the analogy, as autistic. Concerned with herself, her physical recovery, her own fatigue and anxiety, alone and too exhausted to be sociable even when the opportunity arises, she is not the woman she was a few weeks earlier. Exhausted, unrewarded, isolated, overwhelmed by the demands of the baby, often unable to determine what the baby wants, by the end of the first month most mothers feel that the end of their rope is at hand. Ellen said:

> ~ I feel like I'm in some totally spaced-out, private space, and I don't feel like I'll ever get out of it. There's no way I can retain the feeling that I'm in control of this situation.

CHAPTER 2

THE SECOND MONTH
Until I Smile at You

1

AT SOME TIME in the second month the baby smiles a real smile for the first time, and once that happens her mother's feelings about her usually change dramatically. The smile and the other developments of this month turn the baby into a recognizable social being, one fit to participate in a growing range of interactions, some initiated by adults, but many begun by the baby.

The change in a mother's behavior toward her baby and the change in her feelings for the baby happen almost simultaneously. When they occur, the development is unmistakable. At some time during the second month most mothers do begin to love their babies. While it is a rare woman who will admit that she did not love her baby at first but has recently begun to do so, the fact is that in the first month women do not act as if they love their babies, and in the second month most of them do.

Rachel spent most of the first month of her baby's life crying from pain, exhaustion, and loneliness. Her first month was only slightly worse than those of most of the women I interviewed, and the problems that Rachel had were different only in degree, not in kind, from the others'. I saw her for the second time when Matthew was eight weeks old. The change from her disheveled and downcast appearance at our first meeting was dramatic. She was neatly dressed; her hair was brushed. The baby was clean and so was the house. She greeted me smiling.

~ It's just so wonderful and perfect. I love being with him more than anything. I really do spend most of the day just holding him and talking to him. It doesn't even bother me when he cries. I feel much more relaxed with him than I expected to. I just can't imagine life without him. I feel so attached to him; I really hate to be apart from him. I have to confess that when he's asleep, I often just go and get him and let him lie on my stomach.

In the first month Rachel's concern was with herself. The baby was a task, an intrusion into her need for rest and time to recover. Like the other mothers in that first month, she had said very little about him, and when she did mention him she referred to him as "the baby." By the end of the second month she called him by his name, and when he was in the room she carried on our conversation with her gaze fixed, the entire time, on him.

The smile appears in all babies, except the severely brain damaged, at about the same age. There are smiles in the first month, which seem to be smiles of comfort and satisfaction, but it is in the second month that the true social smile is usually first seen. The smile is innate, not learned behavior. Blind babies begin to smile at the same age that sighted babies do, without ever having seen a smile. But without reinforcement, smiling does not persist. Sighted babies smile more and more over the next few months; blind babies smile less and need a great deal of stimulation by voice and by touch in order to continue to smile. Soon after the sighted baby begins to smile, she smiles readily when her mother approaches, and quickly learns that her smile can initiate contact with her mother. But for this development to occur, the baby must be able to see her mother smile.

There are other developments in the second month that are as important as the smile for the burgeoning mother-infant relationship. Around the middle of the month, "the infant," in

44

the words of Daniel Stern, "becomes capable of visually fixating his mother's eyes and holding the fixation with eye widening and eye brightening." This "developmental landmark . . . often catapults the social interaction with mother onto a new level." Her mother's face (or the face of her primary caretaker, who need not be her biological mother, or even a woman for that matter) is most likely to elicit the baby's fixed gaze and her smile. There has been considerable controversy, however, about whether a baby can distinguish one face from another at this age.

Bronson Alcott, the father of Louisa May Alcott and a prominent nineteenth-century educator, was an early student of infant behavior, systematically observing his first-born daughter Anna and keeping copious records of her development. The family's biographer, Madelon Bedell, writes: "At the age of one month, he noted the dawnings of the 'social nature' in a human being, marked by her first smile. The beginnings of intelligence were visible as she moved into the second month and started to distinguish persons from things; to identify individual voices and faces." Like Alcott, careful observers of infant behavior, including many mothers, have always known that babies recognize different people from a very early age. Many experts have insisted, though, that babies could see very little before they were three months old, and that they could not distinguish one individual from another for several months more. As too often happens, women's confidence in their own observations has been undermined by official wisdom. Roger Lewin comments on this phenomenon: "Mothers . . . questioned as to when they thought that their babies could differentiate between them and a stranger, replied, 'in the first couple of weeks, but of course that's not possible.' " The mothers were right, it turns out, as was Bronson Alcott.

Babies discriminate first, it seems, by sense of smell. Aidan Macfarlane, a British pediatrician, conducted experiments to demonstrate babies' abilities in this area. He held a breast pad soaked with the infant's mother's milk to one side of a baby's head and a dry breast pad on the other. By the time they were five days old, the babies would turn their heads toward the milk-soaked pads. By the age of ten days breastfed babies can distinguish the smell of their own mothers' milk from that of another mother, and turn more often toward their own mothers' breast pads than toward those of other lactating women. Within another week or two, infants turn toward their mothers' voices and then to their mothers' faces. By the time smiling and the focused gaze appear, they are most likely to be directed preferentially to the mother, and they are elicited most easily first by her voice and soon after by the sight of her face.

An infant in the second month can produce more gestures and expressions than only the smile. If you stick out your tongue at a baby, she will, within the next ten or fifteen seconds, probably stick hers back out at you; if you grimace, she will try to do the same. This has been shown in a series of experiments in which two-week-old babies were filmed in interactions with adults. The adult would make a gesture — sticking out her tongue or wiggling her fingers — for a few seconds and then wait for a response. Many babies, even at two weeks, were able to respond with imitations.

While we know from experimental evidence that infants prefer to look at the human face over anything else they are likely to encounter, their tendency to mimic suggests other innate abilities. The baby seems to know that she has a face like the one she sees on another person, and without ever having seen her own face, to have a map of it that enables her to imitate facial expressions. She seems to know from the beginning that she is a person like those around her. Adults, too, quite naturally mimic a baby's expressions and sounds, and the French psychoanalyst Jacques Lacan, for one, believes that the mirroring of the baby by those around her is essential for the infant's development of a sense of "self."

When human beings converse, their bodies move precisely in rhythm with each other, both speaker and listener producing a series of nods, twitches, winks, blinks, and body shifts. William Condon and Louis Sander, who have done frame-by-frame analysis of films of adults in conversation, describe both listener and speaker as "moving in tune to the words of the speaker, thus creating a type of dance. The rhythm or tune of the dance is the pattern of speech."

Astonishingly, newborn infants do the dance as well as adults do. Each stressed syllable or pause for breath by the speaker calls forth from the infant a raised eyebrow, a fleeting grimace, a pointing finger or foot. The babies do not react the same way to random tapping or disconnected vowel sounds, but only to language. Condon and Sander found the same responsive pattern in babies listening to a variety of human languages. The infant, then, not only listens to her parents when they speak to her, but months before she will utter her first recognizable word, responds to them in a complex and specifically human way. While the baby's response is not consciously perceived by her mother, it is nonetheless important. Pediatrician T. Berry Brazelton, who has conducted much infant research, believes that "this synchrony becomes the important ambience for their affective communication thereafter. Their communications become a sort of 'mating dance.' "

The question of how and why an infant becomes attached to those around her has been the subject of much investigation, theorizing, and controversy. Freud believed that "love [of the baby for its mother] has origins in attachment to the satisfied need for nourishment." More explicitly, he wrote in *Inhibitions, Symptoms, and Anxiety*: "The infant in arms wants to perceive the presence of its mother . . . only because it already knows by experience that she satisfies all its needs without delay." This is called the secondary drive theory: The infant's need for food is primary; the attachment to mother is secondary, derived from the primary drive. The secondary drive theory is still adhered to by many psychologists and has become to a degree part of the common wisdom of infant development — one of those axioms we know and believe, though we are often unsure of their source.

Many people do believe that babies, like puppies, will come to love best the person who feeds them. But we all know or know of children who desperately love parents who are neglectful, of whom it could not possibly be said that they satisfy all the infant's needs "without delay." Were Freud in fact correct, we might expect the strength of a child's attachment to its mother to be directly proportional to the mother's promptness and perfection in meeting the child's needs, which, fortunately for mothers, is not the case. Nonetheless followers of Freud, including Benjamin Spock (especially in his earliest publications in the 1940s) and John Bowlby, a British psychoanalyst, believed that if a child's needs were not immediately met frustration would result and could lead eventually to neurosis. Many childrearing experts therefore recommended what has become known as "permissive" upbringing, in which the child was (ideally) never frustrated.

Bowlby began to publish his theoretical work on how and why babies form attachments to others in the 1950s. Drawing on the work of the Budapest school of psychoanalysis and the work of ethologists Konrad Lorenz and Harry Harlow, Bowlby departed from his Freudian roots to argue that the secondary drive theory is inadequate to explain attachment and that the infant's tie to its mother stems from a "number of instinctual responses, all of which are primary. . . . Those which I am postulating are sucking, clinging, following, crying, and smiling." All these, as they develop through the baby's first year, are used by the infant to maintain her physical closeness with her mother, a closeness whose evolutionary function was to protect the infant from predators. Now that being eaten by lions is not a pressing danger for most human infants, these primary drives have a more purely social function in establishing the mother-infant relationship.

While Bowlby's list of techniques that the baby has at her disposal for keeping her mother close by, or bringing her back if she has strayed, is a bit limited (since grunts, groans, snuffles, gurgles, vomiting, and bowel movements, to name just a few, will have the same effect), Bowlby must get the credit for making the point that the tie between infant and mother is more social than nutritional.

Studies by Bowlby and others of children in orphanages, sanatoriums, and hospitals have established that one requirement for mental and physical health is an ongoing social and emotional relationship between the child and one or more other people. Institutionalized infants whose physical needs are adequately met by a series of emotionally uninvolved caretakers do not thrive. They are socially, developmentally, and finally physically retarded. Some actually die, even though they have been well fed and kept reasonably clean.

Although the relevance to human beings of research on monkeys is extremely questionable, results of experiments with rhesus monkeys have been applied to questions of child development. Rhesus infants, in a long series of experiments, have been separated from their mothers and kept caged with dummies of various kinds. The baby monkeys get enough to eat, and in some cases a cloth-covered dummy to cling to. Dummy-raised monkeys do not develop normal social relationships with other monkeys; they are aggressive, do not take part in normal play with their peers, are reluctant to mate, and do not properly mother their own infants. Human beings, too, need social and emotional relations for normal development. Babies at a very early age form attachments to fathers, siblings, and others, sometimes in preference to their mothers who feed them. A baby will not form an attachment to an impassive person who simply feeds her, but who offers no emotional sustenance with the food.

Social interplay is not only necessary for babies to form attachments to adults, it is also fundamental to what we, in our culture today, consider proper mothering. We can look at a mother who never plays with or talks to her baby and recognize that she is not, by our standards, a good mother. Maternal responsibility now includes not only keeping a child properly nourished, immunized, disciplined, and educated. Mothers are accountable for every child's being happy, socially well-adjusted, and free from compulsive habits, excessive shyness or aggressiveness, and learning disabilities. (If the problem is not in the way we have raised them, then it is laid to our inadequate prenatal nutrition or smoking or drinking, or to excessive medication that we must have requested during childbirth.)

2

The requirements of motherhood, as we now think of them, are a recent development. Ann Dally, in her excellent study, *Inventing Motherhood*, points out that until recently servants carried a large measure of the responsibility that we now lay to mothers, at least for the middle and upper classes. All but the nearly destitute had *some* help in the home. In the United States, the nanny and the nursery maid disappeared in the 1920s, somewhat earlier than they did in England. With their demise, mothers became responsible for the behavior, as well as the health, of their children. Young mothers, seeking guidance, took up the advice of John Watson in the United States and Truby King in England. Watson, a behaviorist psychologist, believed that conditioning was all that was necessary to raise an acceptable child. He counseled against displays of affection, recommending a handshake at bedtime. He also advocated rigidly scheduled activities, especially feeding, and inveighed against ever rocking or cuddling a distressed infant, since this is only likely to "spoil" him.

That these instructions were as hard to follow as we might imagine is attested to by stories told by our own mothers and grandmothers, and by accounts such as this one from Doris Lessing, who writes of her autobiographical heroine Martha Quest and Martha's best friend Alice, both recently returned home with their newborn infants:

> They would sit, both tense in every nerve, in their sep-
> arate flats, with their eyes on the clock, their breasts tingling
> with milk, while the infants screamed in their cradles for
> an hour, two hours, three hours — until the second hand
> touched the hour, and they might spring up and lift the
> child to be fed.

Both Martha and her friend break down, as many women must have done, feeding the babies at night and eventually putting them on the bottle. The number of women who guiltily and secretly picked up their crying babies to comfort them must run well into the millions. The restrictions, in every case, were presented as being for the good of the child, no matter what the difficulty for the mother. And when the philosophy changed to allow a more permissive style, or to allow mothers, as Spock says, to "follow your instincts," that too was for the child's own good.

A mother's instincts are supposed to, and commonly do, lead her into smiling and gazing and mimicry with her baby. But is the development of a mother's attachment to her child simply "maternal instinct" which is automatic and biologically determined? Maternal instinct does exist in other mammals, where it comprises distinct and well-defined patterns of behavior, each specific to a species, though several species may share similar patterns (cats and rats, for example, both prepare nests in anticipation of the birth of their young). But even in animals, it is not always a simple matter to distinguish the maternal instinct.

J. S. Rosenblatt was able to elicit maternal behavior in male and virgin female rats by placing them with newborn rats. The rats would retrieve the young, lick them, and build nests after prolonged exposure to the baby rats. Rosenblatt believes that the presence of hormones in the mother rat is responsible for her maternal behavior toward the baby rats immediately after they are born and suggests that contact with infants stimulates hormone production in nonmother rats. Hormones may not be the whole answer, though, even in animals. The monkeys who are reared apart from other monkeys, and who therefore have no experience of being mothered by another monkey, do not show normal maternal behavior when they have babies of their own. They will not, for example, pick up and hold their own infants, as a normally reared monkey will. In the monkey, at least, learning is necessary to trigger behavior which is usually thought of as instinctive.

Instinct is even more difficult to distinguish in humans, because any instinct that exists is overlaid with culture, whose customs prescribe appropriate behavior. And while maternal instinct may explain specific behavior patterns in animals, it seems inadequate to explain the genesis of the lasting feelings of attachment that most mothers (and fathers), whether biological or adoptive, form with their children.

Therese Benedek, the psychoanalyst who coined the very evocative term "emotional symbiosis" to describe the early relationship between mother and infant, is one of the few who have considered the relationship from the mother's side. Working from analytic material gathered from patients, Benedek postulates that a woman recapitulates her own infancy and her relationship with her mother once she becomes a mother, because her unconscious holds memories of her own infancy. If the mother's own infancy was comfortable and satisfied, she will try to recreate that experience for her baby. Benedek, following Freud, believes that the tie between a woman and her infant is rooted in the feeding-and-being-fed function. For many mothers, particularly those who breastfeed, feeding the baby does carry a powerful emotional charge — nurturant, protective, and erotic all at once.

But feeding alone does not seem to be enough. Mothers feed their babies, sometimes almost constantly, in the first month, yet few of them report that they feel strongly attached to the babies then. In the second month, the number of feedings per day often drops a bit and the interval between feedings lengthens. Yet it is during this month that most women begin to feel attached. They begin to spend measurably more time with their babies, but they do not spend this time feeding, as we might expect were feeding the source of their positive feelings.

While there has been a torrent of studies on the attachment of infants to their mothers, there has been only one large-scale study to date of the development of mothers' feelings of attachment for their infants. Robson and Moss, the authors of the study, define maternal attachment as "the extent to which a mother feels her infant occupies an essential position in her life." It includes "feelings of warmth, or love, sense of possession, devotion, protectiveness and concern, positive anticipation of prolonged contact, need for and pleasure in continuing transactions." They found that these feelings usually arise during the second month of the baby's life and that they began "in response to the baby's smiling, eye contact, following. . . ." These feelings, fleeting at first, gradually come to dominate most women's relationships with their babies.

For the mother's part, it seems clear that there must be some response from the baby for her to begin to feel attached and to begin to feel like a mother. A woman like Rachel who has been unsmiling and exhausted for more than a month will suddenly start to smile again when the baby does. The caretaking tie, which is formed in the first few weeks, does not by itself afford the mother much satisfaction or enjoyment. But the social tie, initiated by the baby's smiles, gaze, and mimicry, is a potent reward for a mother's caregiving efforts. With the onset of the social tie, the mother's attention begins to turn from herself and her own physical condition to her relationship with the baby. (It is at this point, of course, that most women begin to feel fully recovered from childbirth, so that their physical state is less a concern than it was.) While mothers usually cannot account for the changes in their feelings, they are often sudden and dramatic. Those who have studied the smiling response in infants and the attachment of mothers to infants have noted that within days of the baby's becoming able to focus and the beginning of the development of the social smile, mothers spend measurably more time with their infants, and the extra time is spent in social, not caretaking, activity.

Caregiving alone does not make for an adequate relationship, but it does provide the opportunity for new kinds of exchanges to take place. Typically, at the beginning of a feeding a hungry baby, offered a full breast or bottle, will suck without interruption for several minutes. After this concentrated burst of sucking, she will begin a rhythmic pattern of sucking, stopping briefly, sucking, then stopping for a little longer. The mother holds the baby quite still during the first and later bursts of sucking. During the short pauses she will move slightly, and during the longer pauses she will talk to the baby and smile at her.

The pattern of sucks and pauses is seen in all normal babies and varies only slightly between breast-fed and bottle-fed infants. It is apparently an inborn pattern, and built into this pattern of sucking and resting is an opportunity for mothers (or whoever does the feeding) to interact with their babies, which most of them spontaneously do. Similarly, a baby who is fussing because she wants her diaper changed, and who calms down and smiles as soon as it is removed, is likely to elicit a positive response — smiling and talking — from her mother or whoever is changing her. The baby rather suddenly develops from an organism that seems only to sleep, eat, defecate, and cry to one who smiles at you, looks at you, and is likely to gurgle charmingly with only slight provocation.

3

While mothers spend more time with their babies after the middle of the second month, what else they do is something of a mystery, sometimes even to them. Rachel commented:

〜 My standard of what constitutes a day's activity has lowered so much. When John comes home . . . well, I'm glad he spent the first week with me because he has more of an idea of what you do all day with a baby. Back at work, he's lost it a little bit. So what did I do all day? Well, we managed to walk to the mailbox, and I bought some lettuce, and you know, I can't exactly say what I do all day. He's usually up all day and not quite old enough to really amuse himself, and so he needs to be held a lot. I manage to keep things tidy, and I've written my thank-you notes. I've just started to read the newspaper again. I've worked up to "Dear Abby." I had this fantasy before that somehow this summer was going to be filled with all sorts of productive activity while the baby slept, which of course doesn't happen. In the beginning I got very anxious because I had this list of things I wanted to get done during the day — things around the house, which is obviously falling apart [it wasn't]; a certain amount of work I wanted to get done before school starts; the garden; things I wanted to read — and I don't get any of it done. I realize now — well, intellectually I realize it, emotionally I don't — that those were unrealistic expectations. Staying home to take care of a baby is doing precisely that. A baby takes taking care of. By somebody.

Most women continue to be uninterested in the outside world. Some of the withdrawal seems to be self-protective: Many of the women said that they continued to feel emotionally unsettled and did not want to have to read or hear the usual nightly quota of murders and bombings, to say nothing of kidnappings and cases of child abuse. Several volunteered that they had stopped reading the paper or watching the news on TV, and one woman went so far as to declare, "When Mark brings the paper home, I try to get it into the garbage without seeing the front page. I can't *stand* to know what's going on out there."

There is more to not wanting to know what's going on than simply not reading the newspaper. Most women, unless there is a compelling reason (such as a job) and especially if the baby is their first, still rarely leave the house at this stage. Many are deterred by what seems the enormously complex task of figuring out when and whether the baby might want to eat or sleep, how to get the baby and the carriage down the stairs, whether sun or wind might be too strong. "Do you go out much?" I asked the mother of a seven-week-old girl. "No, not very often," she answered. "Well, you know, sometimes I think I'll take her out when she wakes up, but then she's hungry and then the phone rings, or I'm trying to finish the laundry, and then she's asleep again before I have a chance to get dressed. I don't know . . . I should get out more."

Most of the mothers felt they should be getting out more, either for the sake of the baby (and her need for fresh air) or because they didn't want to appear "lazy," as one expressed it. The skills required to pack up a bottle of juice, an extra diaper, and a sweater in case it gets cold, and to get the carriage or carrier out to the street, are not so formidable that a woman can't manage it all, but the motivation to manage at this stage seems to be lacking for many women. For now, most mothers prefer, if possible, to remain in the nest.

As the attachment to the baby begins to grow, many mothers actually prefer to be alone with their babies. In spite of her loneliness, Rachel was among them:

~ I'm not quite sure why, but it's a mixed blessing having people drop by. Although it's nice to see them, there's something unsatisfying about it. [After a considerable pause, she continued.] I really feel like it disrupts the pattern I've established here. But then I wonder why I'm so wedded to the pattern, because I do get very lonely. Somehow, somebody dropping by for lunch doesn't make me less lonely.

Actually, few people seem to visit new mothers in the second month. The first week or two after the baby's birth is the customary time for visitors; after that, they usually need to be invited. In addition to feeling unable to get out with the baby, many mothers still feel uneasy about leaving the baby with anyone else. Rachel and her husband had gone out together for the first time without the baby when he was just eight weeks old. The following day, I asked her how she felt about leaving him.

⤳ Well, the sitter was a woman who lives right close by, and who's our close friend, and we went to see a revival of *Casablanca*, which is one of my favorite movies, so it kept my interest, except that I did keep thinking about Matthew. I got very nervous, and I really didn't like that at all. I can't stand leaving him with somebody else, and thinking about doing it in September [when she planned to return to her job] makes me terribly anxious. Part of it is not knowing who the person will be, but I just imagine terrible things about the person. I assume I'm going to get somebody I like and trust. If I don't . . . I mean I'm not going to leave him with somebody I *don't* like and trust, but I just can't imagine such a person existing, so that's why I keep getting anxious.

Ellen, who had to return to work when Daniel was two months old, said to me the week before she went back, "I've interviewed four people to take care of him. I didn't like any of them. I don't know what I'm going to do. I just don't feel like I'm ready for this. I'm really a wreck over it."

Taken together, the mother's difficulty in getting out with the baby, the diminished number of visitors, and the reluctance to leave the baby with anyone else add up to the mother's being alone in the house with the baby most of the time, especially if the baby is the first. This may seem a grim situation, and for some women it is certainly so. For many, though, for a few weeks, it is a honeymoon. Alone with a new love, the mother gets a chance to get acquainted, to learn the baby's responses and rhythms and patterns without interference or interruption, a chance to indulge her feelings and to spend her days doing things that she knows would look ridiculous to an outsider. This period can perhaps be enjoyed best by women who know it will not last forever; women who have, as both Rachel and Ellen did, a forseeable end point to the isolation — in both their cases, a return to an outside job. And the honeymoon can be enjoyed *only* by those women whose lives and personalities permit its relative inactivity. Not all women have the opportunity.

Alice, a graduate student in psychology, gave birth to Maya, her second child, at the Maternity Center in New York, where family-centered maternity care is provided by nurse-midwives to low-risk patients. By the time Maya was ten days old, Alice was already voicing the kind of complaint that the first-time mothers didn't have until the second month: "Feeding the baby, making the bed, getting dinner takes up the whole day," she said. She sounded weary just talking about it. Alice, who is black, also mentioned matter-of-factly that she also had to care for her three-year-old son, that her husband had been unable to get time off from work, and that the baby was not born in the middle of final exams only because she arrived three weeks late.

Having had the baby at the Maternity Center, Alice had come home a few hours after the delivery and after that had little chance to rest. By the middle of the second month it was obvious that her attachment to the baby was rather different from Rachel's. Alice said, "There's a lot less romance with the second, though I feel much more comfortable with her than I did with Kareem. With him, everything was new and wonderful. Now I find myself waiting for her to *do* something."

In many respects, Alice had got off to a very good start with Maya. Labor and delivery, while Alice described it as "very rough," was also extremely short. Her recovery, except for two days of uterine contractions during feedings and sore nipples that responded promptly to the application of warm compresses, was quick. The baby was not demanding. Her husband, when he was at home, was "really helpful. He puts out one hundred percent," she said. But Alice had no time for a honeymoon. The baby had been carefully timed to arrive at the beginning of the summer. By midsummer, when the baby was six weeks old, Alice was taking full advantage of her "free time." While she felt pressed by having to find the time for housework, marketing, errands, and two children, the struggle to maintain a schedule and fit everything into it was being won. Alice even found time every afternoon to take a two-hour exercise class while her son played with a neighbor's child and the baby slept.

A second or later baby probably has to try a little harder. Her smile has to be a little brighter and her babbling a little louder to attract her mother's attention. Maya, however, was doing her part and beginning to succeed in captivating her mother.

～ Last night, Kareem was already asleep, and Maya and I had a "conversation" that went on for about fifteen minutes. I had forgotten how wonderful that sort of stuff is when it starts to happen. The complete rapture of the first one isn't there, but I am finding now that I enjoy her much more.

There is, of course, never another quite like the first, though second babies, as Alice pointed out, have the advantage of producing much less anxiety in their parents than first ones do. And, with the second, mothers have no choice but to be organized, since the older child or children simply cannot be ignored, meals must be prepared, and the older child cannot be expected to sit in the house day after day; he must be taken out, unless he is old enough to go out alone. If Alice had any desire to isolate herself, she could not indulge it. The demands on her were too pressing, the "free time" of the summer too short, the overwhelming newness of motherhood, which Rachel just wanted to sit and relish, was missing.

4

Not every first-time mother becomes passionately attached to her baby by the end of the second month. Even if the new mother has few responsibilities besides the baby, the woman saddled with an infant who cries a lot and sleeps only a little usually finds her very hard to love. Since the mother's feelings of attachment depend so much on the development of the social relationship, the attachment does not usually develop as long as the baby remains a screaming infant. Robson and Moss note in their study of attachment formation that excessive crying is one of the prime reasons for delayed attachment. And Michael Lewis and Leonard Rosenblum, in *The Effect of the Infant on Its Caregiver*, write that "attachment *decreases* [emphasis mine] in some mothers after the first month if crying, fussing, and other demands for physiological caregiving do not decrease as they do in most infants." Mothers also seem, logically enough, to be most enthusiastic about the baby who cries little and whose social repertoire develops early, although it would be hard to prove that mothers become attached to their babies exactly in inverse proportion to the amount of time the baby spends crying. The baby's crying, in the second month, is going to be one of the major factors in her developing relationship with her mother.

All babies, of course, cry. The average baby cries for a total of about two hours a day, usually in short bursts. There are some who do most of their crying all at once, most often at the end of the afternoon. There are babies who, for no apparent reason, cry much more than the average, and there are those who suffer from colic and seem to cry all the time.

An infant's crying seems to be designed, in evolutionary terms, to be annoying to adults. It is, for a time at least, the baby's most efficient signal, the one most likely to bring a response and get her what she needs. Thus crying occupies a good deal of a mother's attention. It occupies the attention of the child care experts as well, and they all seem to have strong opinions about crying, what it means, and what should be done about it. There is little argument today about the correct response to a baby who cries because of hunger. Experts and mothers alike have largely abandoned rigid feeding schedules, and it is now rare for a hungry baby to be allowed to cry for much longer than it takes to prepare something to satisfy her. There is a consensus that hungry babies should be fed and that sleeping babies need not be wakened simply in order to eat.

There has never been much controversy about responding to a baby who is in pain. Child care books have always been filled with remedies for colic, for instance, and mothers are not advised to let the colicky baby "cry it out," until the various treatments have been tried and found ineffective.

The continuing controversy over crying concerns crying with no immediately obvious cause. The pendulum of fashion has, over the centuries, swung between the extremes of *never* responding to the crying baby and *always and immediately* responding to her. The prescription has to do, as a rule, with the writer's philosophical view of the baby, rather than with his understanding of infant psychology. Where Rousseau saw the child as intrinsically good and therefore deserving of a positive response which could best bring out the goodness, the American colonists saw the child as the bearer of original sin, in need of strict discipline from birth to grow into an upright Christian.

Within our own century there has been a radical change in belief and behavior in response to infant crying. The best-selling U.S. Children's Bureau pamphlet, *Infant Care,* in its first edition in 1914, classifies crying as a "bad habit," and advises the mother that "when a baby cries simply because he has learned from experience that this brings him what he wants, it is one of the worst habits he can learn." The author, Mrs. Max West, like most of her contemporaries, is a firm believer in early training and discipline to establish control over the infant as soon as possible after it is born.

L. Emmett Holt, author of the popular *The Care and Feeding of Children*, which was first published in 1894 and went through eight editions by 1916, wrote:

> *What is the cry of indulgence or from habit?* This is often heard even in very young infants, who cry to be rocked, to be carried about, sometimes for a light in the room, for a bottle to suck, or for the continuance of any other bad habit which has been acquired. *How can we be sure that a child is crying to be indulged?* If it stops immediately when it gets what it wants, and cries when it is withdrawn or withheld.

By the early 1940s there had been a revolution in attitudes. Babies, the precious hope of a nation at war, deserved every possible indulgence.

> Babies [wrote Dorothy V. Whipple in 1944] do not cry for nothing. They cry because of some need. You will never spoil a baby by attending to his needs. A baby needs food and warmth; but he also needs love and all the little baby things that go with his mother's demonstration of her love. A baby who gets plenty of this kind of attention will not cry for more. It is the baby who has never had enough who is always crying for more. *He* is the spoiled baby.

In its first edition in 1946, Spock's *Baby and Child Care* very much reflected the tenor of those times. He repeatedly counseled mothers to rely on their instincts:

> When he cries it's for a good reason — maybe it's hunger, or wetness, or indigestion, or just because he's on edge and needs soothing. The baby's cry is there to call you. The uneasy feeling you have when you hear him cry is meant to be part of your nature, too. A little gentle rocking may

actually be good for him. Meanwhile, be natural and comfortable and enjoy your baby.

By 1957, a more conservative time, Spock was willing to be a little more hard-hearted. By then, his "rule of thumb" was:

> If a baby has been crying hard for 15 minutes or more and if it's more than 2 hours after the last feeding — or even if it's less than 2 hours after a *very small* feeding — give him another feeding. . . . If it's less than 2 hours after a *full* feeding, it's unlikely that he's hungry. Let him cry for 15 or 20 minutes more.

Spock doesn't say what to do then, nor does he offer much comfort to the mother, watching the clock and wringing her hands and wondering what to do when it's exactly two hours after a middle-sized feeding. Spock seems to have forgotten entirely his own earlier counsel that the baby might simply need soothing.

By the early 1970s, once again a more liberal time, the experts had again changed their tack, and a popular work, Dr. Lee Salk's *What Every Child Would Like His Parents to Know*, advised:

> You certainly should pick up your baby if he cries for more than a few moments, like when he is turning over in his sleep. . . . I myself feel it is impossible to spoil an infant. The concept of spoiling just does not apply to babies under the age of nine or ten months, since they are utterly dependent, completely incapable of satisfying their own needs, and absolutely unable to put off any gratification without some sense of frustration. They require the cooperation of adults to be satisfied. You won't spoil your baby by helping him.

And Klaus and Kennell in 1976 awarded the maximum score of three points to the mothers in their studies who picked up the babies whenever they cried.

Silvia Bell and Mary Ainsworth studied the actual (rather than reported) behavior of mothers in response to their infants' crying by sending observers into the homes. The observers recorded both the babies' and the mothers' activities in several visits over the space of a year. They found that if the mother responded quickly and consistently to the baby's crying in the first three months of life, the baby would cry less in the next three months. This result was consistent throughout the first year; that is, if the mother responded promptly in the second three-month period, the baby cried less in the third three months, and so on. By the time the baby is a year old, those who "have well-developed channels of communication tend to be the same ones who cry little and . . . these are the ones whose cries were promptly heeded throughout the first year of life." By contrast, "from the beginning of the first year, maternal ignoring [of infant crying] in one quarter is correlated significantly with a higher frequency of infant crying in the following quarter." So, at least according to one study, it is worthwhile responding to a baby's cries, while ignoring her in an attempt not to "spoil" her is apparently self-defeating.

The problem of how to cope with a crying baby is most urgent, of course, when the baby cries all the time, as some colicky babies do. Parents of colicky babies are usually the recipients of a good deal of advice, some of which may be helpful. Colic has frequently been attributed to the *mother's* anxiety and insecurity, but no study has ever shown it to be anything but a digestive disorder of babies, which, while it may well *cause* stress in the mother, is not caused by it.

Colic usually appears around the age of three weeks (when most babies become more irritable) and almost always ends by the age of three months, although there are some unhappy parents whose babies suffer full-blown colic for up to six months. The symptoms of colic are unmistakable: The infant's belly is distended; she pulls her legs up sharply; she burps or passes gas rectally; and always, she screams. In some babies the attacks occur for only part of the day, usually in the evening. In others,

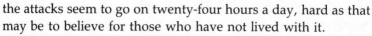

the attacks seem to go on twenty-four hours a day, hard as that may be to believe for those who have not lived with it.

Elaine, whose two-month-old baby stopped crying only when he was being pushed along in his carriage, talked to me one day while the baby was being aired by a sitter.

∽ He just cries and cries; we do everything we can think of, and he just keeps crying. We hold him over our knees. We put him over a hot water bottle. We wrap a band around his belly. We've given him spearmint tea, chamomile tea, angelica tea and catnip tea. I've stopped eating all but the blandest foods. I feel so totally helpless. The baby just keeps crying and everyone tells you it'll end when he's three months old, but that's a month away and I don't know how I'm going to take it. Another month is thirty more nights. I don't even like him anymore.

The benefits of even an ideal delivery or a bonding period in the first hour or plenty of rest postpartum cannot outweigh the damage that can be done to the relationship between mother and baby by weeks upon weeks of exhausted management of a colicky infant. A baby who is genuinely ill usually arouses pity, anxiety, and as much loving care as can be provided, but one with colic, who howls lustily from sundown to sunup and then, after a brief rest, cries again all day, who seems not to eat at all, but gains well, and keeps her family from a peaceful meal or a night's rest for weeks on end is very hard to love. The attachment between such a baby and her parents is often inhibited until the colic passes.

A baby with colic, like any other, benefits from having a calm, relaxed caretaker, but the mother of a colicky infant is rarely that. The distress caused by trying unsuccessfully to relieve the baby's discomfort usually outweighs whatever satisfaction might otherwise be gained from the fact that these babies usually gain weight steadily and are otherwise healthy.

Caretaking in cases like these entirely dominates the relationship, and little else develops until the colic passes and the mother has a chance to notice that the baby has suddenly, it seems, developed a whole set of rather charming social skills. Until that time, she may feel as Elaine did: "I feel like I don't really know how it feels to be a mother. I just feel like a machine who takes care of a baby."

Even when the baby is normally healthy, the attachment may not be established in the second month if the mother cannot allow herself to enjoy the relationship, at least a little. While a feeling of responsibility is one essential element of attachment, it can also overwhelm the mother and interfere. Because the advice from the experts (such as Salk's, "You certainly should pick up your baby if he cries for more than a few moments") is invariably addressed to mothers — or at least is most readily taken to heart by mothers — many women internalize a standard of perfection that no one could possibly attain. Anne, who had a two-month-old daughter and a three-year-old son, sat rocking the baby and talking to me:

> ~ I find myself going to bed every night thinking about whether I've been a good mother that day, and if I've made Ben cry, or if I've let the baby cry too much. I run through my head and think: "What did I do? What didn't I do?" I don't think Vince [her husband] goes through that kind of torture. I feel like I'm constantly needing help, and it's difficult asking for help from Vince. If I do, it makes me feel I'm not doing something I should be doing.

The sense of responsibility, when carried to an extreme as it was for Anne, or unrelieved caretaking like that faced by Elaine with her colicky baby, can delay the development of attachment. Gazing at the baby is a prime sign of attachment. Anne and Elaine scarcely looked at their babies, even while holding them.

Carmen was another mother who never seemed to look at her baby. Carmen's baby had been delivered by a resident at a large municipal hospital after three days of labor. He was her second boy, a bitter disappointment, and she refused to hold him on the delivery table. Remorseful and afraid, then, when the baby was taken to the intensive care unit, she asked for permission to see and hold him, but was told that only hospital personnel were permitted in the infant ICU. On the second day, she was allowed to hold him for a few minutes. On the third day after delivery, Carmen returned home without the baby, still not sure why he was in intensive care, afraid there was something seriously wrong with him that the doctors would not tell her, wondering whether her baby would even survive. A day later she returned to the hospital to be told that the baby was perfectly healthy and that she could take him home. After another four-hour wait while a pediatrician was sought to discharge him, Carmen took the baby home.

Carmen eventually learned that the baby had been kept in the ICU only because her waters had broken early in her very long labor and that infection in the newborn sometimes occurs in such circumstances. Carmen didn't question the hospital staff's medical judgment, but even two months later she was justifiably furious at the disrespect and insensitivity they had shown in refusing to explain what they were doing and why.

Carmen never referred to the baby by name, calling him "the baby" or "this one," to distinguish him from her older boy. Most mothers, for the first month or so, refer to the baby as "the baby." It is usually not until some time in the second month, or even the third, that the baby achieves enough separate identity in her mother's mind to require being called by name. In cases where, for whatever reason, the attachment is not established early, the baby remains "the baby," sometimes until the sixth month or occasionally, as with one woman I interviewed, even longer. But like a woman with a new lover, a mother, once she feels attached to the new baby, likes to mention her name.

Carmen's low-keyed response to her baby at two months was, I believe, the result of the enforced and unnecessary separation from him in the hospital. (More enlightened institutions today allow parents to see and hold their babies whenever they wish, no matter how sick the infant or how uncertain its chances of survival.) Carmen had no baby to interpose between herself and her disappointment at not having a daughter, no infant toward whom she could feel protective in those first important days. Unsure of his state and his survival, she had no motivation to love him and every reason to protect herself from overwhelming grief and guilt if he died.

Her baby at two months of age was a "good baby." He slept and ate on schedule, leaving Carmen time to devote to her older child. She spent little time with the baby that was not required by his immediate needs, but he had started to smile, and the stage was being set for the beginning of an attachment.

> ~ I enjoy him now, and we play together more than we used to. I'm more comfortable with him. When I came home, I didn't remember anything about babies, but then everything came back to my mind, and I take care of him now like a regular baby. I want to go back to work [which she planned to do when the baby was five months old], because I think it's much better for me to be away, but something else is in my mind, like I don't want to be away from the baby.

Carmen's weak attachment reflected itself as insecurity about her competence as a mother. In spite of having raised one child, she worried: "Sometimes I think I'm doing everything right, but most of the time I don't have confidence in myself about being a mother."

Kate, who had a two-month-old daughter, was another woman who responded in the negative when I asked if she thought she was a good mother: "Probably not. There are times when I really lose patience, and I don't feel like feeding her, like at the fourth feeding in a four-hour period."

Every mother loses patience once in a while, and hardly anyone would blame a mother for not enjoying having to nurse her baby hourly. But the mothers who were securely attached to their babies, while they talked about losing patience and resenting the baby's demands at times, didn't make these things add up to being a bad mother. I asked Kate when she had begun feeling attached to the baby, and she replied:

~ I don't think I've ever got a feeling of being connected to her. I guess when she starts to smile I do, because that's something, you know, we share that, but not very much. At one point, I didn't know if I was going to have any feelings about her. But now I don't mind her at all.

Kate was a diabetic and because of that condition had delivered by Caesarean section. I asked whether she'd had general anesthesia.

~ Well, I didn't, but I was supposed to. It didn't work. The great anesthesiologist that we waited hours for screwed up, and they started the whole thing while I was conscious. Finally, the sodium pentothal got to me, and I went half asleep, and then I had dreams, which you're not supposed to either. You're supposed to be so far under that you can't dream. Awful, awful dreams. That happened after they cut me open. First, they didn't give enough, and second, they didn't wait long enough for it to take effect. I couldn't talk because I had a tube down my throat, and you're all tied down, so you can't let anybody know you're awake. Finally I passed out, but that was after I felt them ripping the baby out. I had this horrible dream, and then I passed out, and the next thing I was in the recovery room, with Jim saying, "You have a girl," and I wasn't at all interested in that. And he said, "Do you want to see her?" And I said, "Not right now."

After this brilliant start, Kate saw the baby once on the day after she was born. Then, because Kate was running a slight fever, the baby was kept in the nursery for another full day.

~ I got very upset that they wouldn't bring the baby in, because by that time I wanted to see her. My internist, who's a diabetic specialist, came in and said I had postpartum depression, because I was crying. I was crying because they wouldn't bring me the baby. I got the resident on duty to acknowledge that I didn't have a lung problem, because the only thing they're really concerned about is transmitting respiratory infections. So he wrote on the chart that, even though I wasn't supposed to feed her, I could get the baby. So I had her for three feedings. The next morning, the pediatrician came in, and he said to me, "You can't have the baby; it's a Board of Health rule." I was just so infuriated. The resident was not hiding behind this Board of Health rule, but the big doctor was. So I had to wait another twenty-four hours to get the baby. I was anxious to feel connected to her. That's why I wanted them to bring her to me, so I could look at her. And feel something.

Kate had analyzed her situation:

~ I think I'm particularly disconnected from her because I associate her with the nightmares I had under the drug. I find that I fall back into them. The dream was that I was being tricked. Because I *was* being tricked, because I was told before I went into the delivery room that I would be out, and I wouldn't feel anything. So I was tricked. And the dream was all about how I was being tricked. So I feel that part of my relationship to her is clouded by the fact that I think I'm still being tricked somehow. I just can't figure it out.

Elaine and Anne, Carmen and Kate were women who were late, or later than average, in forming an attachment to their babies. Elaine had a baby who screamed all the time. Anne was overburdened by the responsibility for two small children, a reluctance to ask for help from her husband, and a tendency to be too severe in judging her own behavior. Carmen and Kate both had lengthy separations from their babies, and those separations had the effect, predicted by some of the researchers, of interfering with their feelings about the babies.

Separation from the baby does not necessarily cause delayed attachment; there were women who had very strong attachments to their babies by the age of two months in spite of two or three days of almost complete separation. Carmen and Kate, however, both had experiences which, combined with separation, exacerbated its effects. For Carmen there was her disappointment in the baby's sex, as well as her fear that there was something wrong with him; for Kate, the nightmare of the Caesarean section. Each of these four was aware that her feelings for the baby were rather mild, and that positive feelings were, at best, fleeting. Anne and Carmen, both of whom had older children, both remarked that the first baby was much more exciting and that their emotions had been much more intense the first time around. While that is not an unusual observation for mothers of second babies, both these mothers made a great point of the difference between the two experiences. Compared to Rachel and some of the others, these four mothers at the end of the second month seemed rather neutral about their babies.

But neutrality was not to be a permanent condition. Elaine started to like her baby the moment he stopped screaming, which happened when he was almost three months old, though at first she was a bit reluctant to get involved:

> ∾ For about a month, every time he started to cry, I froze. I thought, "Oh God, he isn't going to stop." But he did, and eventually I got some confidence that he would stop, and he was just a normal baby. I also learned that there were things I could do that would make him stop crying, which there weren't when he had the colic. And he smiles, and he's just so *cute*.

Anne's attachment to her baby improved most markedly, by her own account, when the baby was almost six months old and Anne returned to graduate school. In spite of the pressures she faced, she found that the limited time she had to spend with the baby was tremendously enjoyable, once she established a schedule and learned the routine:

> ~ I enjoy her now in a way that I just didn't when I was home all the time. It's hard to explain why. I guess it's that I've set aside a little time when I'm doing nothing but be with her, so that's what I'm doing. When I was with her all the time, I always felt like there was something else — being with Ben [her son] or my husband, or the housework or the cooking — that I really should be doing. Now there's less time, but I'm clearer on what it's for.

Anne felt better about herself, interested and involved in her work, and felt that she had more to give to her children when she returned to them at the end of the day. She also stopped chastising herself nightly for every little lapse that she had made during the day, as she had done when the baby was younger and she was at home all the time. She apparently needed to separate herself somewhat from her mothering role to begin to be able to enjoy it and her children. She had arranged for the essential ingredient: Her son was in a good day-care center, and the baby was cared for by a woman she liked and trusted. Anne was thus relieved of some of the anxiety that beset her when she felt she had to be "on duty" twenty-four hours a day.

Both Carmen and Kate came to feel love and connection to their babies, although these feelings did not develop fully for another two or three months. In the meantime, their babies formed attachments with other members of the family. While the mother is usually the handiest partner around for a baby's social and emotional exchanges, it need not be the mother who fills the role. It is rare for a mother and baby to be so isolated that no one else is available to be partner to the infant if the mother is not inclined to do it herself. Even when the mother is present and responsive, babies quite often turn out to be most attached to someone else or to form several attachments simultaneously. Rudolph Schaffer and Peggy Emerson found, in fact, that 29 percent of the infants they studied formed several attachments. Fathers, siblings, grandparents, friends, and caretakers are all, according to Schaffer, good candidates.

For example, while I was interviewing Carmen, the baby woke from his nap. Carmen's older son, who was five, came in and asked his mother if he could get the baby. The baby stopped crying as soon as he saw his brother, and I could hear the two of them laughing, the older boy talking and the baby cooing in response. The older boy brought the baby into the kitchen, where his mother and I were talking, and soon the baby was lying on a blanket on the floor while his brother and a cousin who lived nearby played with and around him. Later, when Carmen picked up the baby to feed him, I noticed that the baby's reaction to her was extremely subdued when compared to the liveliness of his response to his brother. Since one of the few possible measures of attachment at the age of two months is the "lighting up" that the baby does when confronted by different people, from the evidence before me it seemed that this baby had a stronger attachment to his brother, who was his playmate, than he did to his mother.

In the first days after Kate's return from the hospital, while she was still recovering from her Caesarean and its accompanying nightmares, Kate's daughter formed a very strong relationship with her father and with a number of Kate's friends, who began coming to help out. Those relationships may have provided the stimulation that the baby needed and was not yet getting from her mother. Kate was a magazine editor who had planned to get back to work as soon as possible. Given her mild feelings about the baby, I assumed that she would return to her job as soon as she was physically able after the delivery. I was wrong. While she had taken the baby to the office a couple of times, she was not working, nor was she trying very hard to find someone who would take care of the baby when she did. Kate was actually quite withdrawn. She said:

~ I'm getting placid, I think. More placid and more accepting than I would be normally. I'm less interested in seeing people, even though I've never been particularly social, so it's hard to make comparisons. I've always been content not to see people for periods of time, but I think I'm more that way now.

Kate, like many of the other first-time mothers, preferred to stay at home alone with the baby. Whatever the reasons were for Kate's lack of interest in seeing other people or in returning immediately to her job, it had the effect of keeping her alone with the baby so that their relationship had the necessary environment in which to develop. Contact with the baby seems to be the essential factor in the development of the mother's feelings of love for her infant. Able to be alone, Kate learned to love her.

CHAPTER 3

THE THIRD AND FOURTH MONTHS

Symbiosis

> I recall the time when, suckling each
> of my children, I saw his eyes full open
> to mine, and realized each of us was
> fastened to the other, not only through
> mouth and breast, but through our
> mutual gaze: the depth, calm, passion
> of that dark blue, maturely focused
> look.
> — ADRIENNE RICH, *Of Woman Born*

1

ON THE DAY that Molly was two months old I woke and sat up in bed, thinking, "I have work to do." I am not sure that I would have chosen to resume work at that point, had I been free to make the choice, but I was not, and whether the urgency I felt came from within myself or from a publisher's deadline, it was there. Molly at that age would lie quietly, chatting at her mobile for an hour or more, and I was sure I could take advantage of her good nature and work while she was nearby. I soon discovered, however, that I could not.

The first day I placed the carriage in which she lay near my work table, so that I could see her without getting up. I spent the morning gazing at her, the typewriter humming unattended behind me. The next day I moved the carriage a few feet away, so as not to be so easily distracted, but the temptation to walk over to it, to see the smile that would light her face when she saw me, was irresistible. She would gurgle and I would gurgle back. If I walked away, she would coo softly and I would return, and the glorious baby smile would burst forth again.

After that second morning I set about finding a reliable person who would care for her a few mornings a week (at the sitter's house, not mine) so that I could write. For the next few months I managed to work at home between Molly's eight AM and noon feedings. When she got home we would resume our "conversation." I remember, too, the afternoons during those same months, sitting in the park talking to friends, my eyes locked with Molly's.

The state she and I were in then is called *symbiosis*. It is the most intense and the most uncomplicated attachment I have ever felt for another human being. Months later, when I again tried to write with Molly in the house, the interruptions came from the need to watch her so that she didn't get hurt, or from her wanting someone to play with, or from feedings or changings or outings to the park. I was still unable to work while she was around, but no longer did I hang over her crib, gazing at my sleeping infant, or if she was awake, engage in cooing matches, reluctant to pull myself away and unable to concentrate on anything when I did.

Symbiosis, which begins by the time the baby is two months old and reaches its peak before she is five months old, has been described by psychologist Margaret Mahler as a state of "dual unity." The term is borrowed from biology, where it refers to a close association of two different organisms "that may be but is not necessarily of benefit to each." "Symbiosis," Mahler writes, "describes that state of undifferentiation, of fusion with mother, in which the 'I' is not yet differentiated from the 'not-I' and in which inside and outside are only gradually coming to be sensed as different." The infant does not yet recognize that her mother is a separate person, but experiences her mother as an extension of herself, one which fills her needs and gratifies her wishes.

While symbiosis has only been used to describe the baby's

view of the world, it is also a useful metaphor to represent the mother's sense of the state of affairs. A mother, in the symbiotic phase, still feels that the baby is very much a part of herself. The infant feels that she and her mother constitute a single entity, and her mother feels much the same. This is not a hallucination; the ties that bind the two are real and complicated. On the simplest physiological level the mother's breasts fill, sometimes uncomfortably, when the baby whimpers, and it is the baby's suckling that can relieve the pressure. Mothers wake at the baby's slightest stirring, a phenomenon so well recognized that Freud coined the term *Mutterschlaffen* to describe this easily disturbed sleep. Because mothers commonly spend more time with their babies than anyone else does, they tend to be better interpreters of the baby's signals than anyone else is. And because the mother thus tends to be most responsive to the baby, the baby is often particularly responsive to her. Many mothers, when they are away from their babies during this period, find themselves distracted from what they are doing by their longing for the baby. They need the response, the special smile that is theirs alone. At the same time, paradoxically, mothers are capable of forgetting the baby. Sarah was one of several mothers who described very similar incidents:

> ‿﹏ I met a friend for lunch the other day for the first time. We spent about two hours at the restaurant, talking, having a great time. I talked about Jake some at the beginning, but as we came out of the restaurant, I suddenly realized I had not thought about Jacob *once* for over an hour. Not just not thinking about him, but it was like he never existed at all. It made me feel very free.

Later on, mothers don't forget babies in this absolute way, and I can only guess why they do (and fairly often, if I am to believe them) during the symbiotic phase. It may be because the baby does not yet have much separate identity or reality, as far as her mother is concerned. The mothers still seem to experience the babies as extensions of themselves, and forgetting the baby is akin to not consciously remembering that you have a nose, or shoulders. It's so *there* you can ignore it altogether. Later, when the baby is more definitely a separate person, she has more reality and is impossible to forget.

The symbiotic phase is necessary for the development of the mother as we know her and the development of a child in a fashion that we consider normal. Eye contact is, in our culture, one of the hallmarks of the healthy symbiotic relationship. Psychologists like Margaret Mahler and poets like Adrienne Rich frequently remark on the intensity of that gazing. It is, however, to some degree a culturally determined phenomenon.

In cultures where the baby is carried all the time by her mother (or someone else), there is usually a minimum of eye-to-eye contact between mother and infant. A baby carried on her mother's back who is fed while being held upright against the mother's chest (as millions of babies in other cultures are), does not have the opportunity for mutual gazing with the mother that we consider essential. The function of mutual gazing and mimicry, which is to make the baby gradually aware of herself and her similarity to and separateness from other human beings, may in other cultures be served by skin-to-skin contact (which our babies get little of) and the development of tactile, rather than visual and aural, sensitivity. (The anthropologists I. DeVore and Melvin Konner have also noted that among the !Kung, a hunter-gatherer people of the Kalahari who carry their babies in hip slings, older children, and especially young girls, often run over to the infant and have short but lively "conversations.")

It is during the symbiotic phase that most mothers and babies settle into a particular dyadic rhythm. Together they establish a schedule, and the mother learns and adjusts to the baby's patterns. Feedings become more regular; the baby gets hungry at predictable times. She comes to recognize the preparations for feeding: being picked up or changed, the sight or sound of a bottle being filled. Knowing that she is going to be fed, she may get excited and wave her arms or legs, or vocalize, or cry. The breastfeeding mother often feels her milk let down at the baby's first cry of hunger, or even a few seconds or minutes before it. Sleep, too, becomes more regular for mother and baby. The baby begins to sleep and wake at the same times every day, and her pattern more or less gradually begins to conform to that of the family, so that she sleeps more at night and is awake more during the day. Her daytime sleep will in time become a morning and an afternoon nap. When asleep she is more firmly asleep, and her brain wave patterns show that both her deep sleep and her dreaming sleep are much like that of adults. She is awake for longer periods, and she is more fully alert. The somnolent state of the early weeks, which is sometimes difficult to characterize as either sleeping or waking, is less frequent.

The mother adjusts physically to the baby's sleep and waking patterns. No longer wakened every hour or two, she begins to sleep longer and more deeply, and her fatigue begins to lift. If the baby's sleep habits do not improve during this period (and many do not), the mother's continuing fatigue can precipitate a severe and continuing depression. Instead of feeling more in tune and closer with the baby, she may become increasingly alienated and distant.

The baby's signals in this period become clearer, and the mother's ability to understand them (a result of both the baby's growing competence and the mother's greater familiarity with her) improves. The baby learns to deliver a host of signals — for hunger, fatigue, boredom, physical discomfort, pain, and loneliness. The baby tired of lying in one position will begin to fuss and move around. Her mother, hearing her, seeing her squirming helplessly, recognizes or empathizes with her discomfort and, having learned by now that the baby sometimes likes to lie on her back for a while, turns her over. The baby then smiles in thanks, and mother and baby both feel comfortable and satisfied.

It may be too easy, however, to overemphasize a mother's

ability to read her baby's cues. There are studies of the sounds and rhythms of the cries that babies produce to indicate hunger and pain and fatigue. Several years ago, I heard an advertisement for a long-playing record designed to help mothers understand the different cries. The new mother could listen to the record in her spare time, as if learning French. (It was not explained why any mother would spend more time than absolutely necessary listening to crying babies.) Sarah, the mother of a three-month-old son, had suffered agonies of inexperience when Jacob was one month old, but now she said, "He's saved himself by being more or less on a schedule. People keep telling me, 'Oh, you'll learn to recognize his cries,' but I don't. He starts to cry and I look at the clock and say, 'Well, he must be hungry.' "

The infant's memory begins to develop from the time she is born. The ability to remember precedes the ability to recognize; a mental image of an object or person must persist from one occasion of seeing it to the next in order for the object to be recognized as being the same as the one that was there before. While an infant's motor skills can be measured directly, her ability to remember and recognize is inferred, usually from her response to changes in familiar things. Thus if, as was done in one experiment, a stranger's voice is made to issue apparently from the mother's mouth and the baby gets upset, we can conclude that the baby can remember her mother's voice well enough to be disturbed if the voice she hears is different. Similar experiments and parents' observations have shown that babies, from a very early age, recognize and remember familiar faces and voices, the position in which they are usually held, their favorite places — a bed, crib, or infant seat — and the smell and taste of their mother's milk or their accustomed formula.

By the end of the third month, a baby can see as well as an adult. "The infant can track the mother as she leaves, approaches and moves about the room. His communicative network is thus vastly extended," writes Harvard researcher Daniel Stern. The baby can now carry on a "conversation" with the mother even when she is not standing right in front of the baby. But what many mothers discover is that for these few months, as soon as the baby begins to smile or to converse, the mother is inexorably drawn to approach the baby, to continue the conversation, and so to extend and deepen the relationship.

In an article titled, "Early Attempts at Speech," Colwyn Trevarthen writes: "Human intelligence develops from the start as an interpersonal process, and the maturation of consciousness . . . is a product rather than an ingredient of this process, a consequence rather than a cause of understanding between persons." Poet Adrienne Rich, in *Of Woman Born*, writes: "It's as if in the mother's eyes, her smile, her stroking touch, the child first reads the message: You are there!" The baby now begins to learn that she is a person much like those around her, able in her own way to do the same things.

"The mother too," Rich continues, "is discovering her self newly." During the symbiotic period, a time of intense and extensive mutual exchange between mother and infant, the mimicry and mirroring which began when the baby first smiled becomes more elaborate. The infant, with better perceptual abilities and increased motor control, becomes increasingly skilled, a more fitting partner for her mother. It is in this period that mothers begin to say, "I can see that she's becoming a real person."

It is self-evident that *being* a mother depends on the presence of a child. But *feeling* like a mother depends on that same interpersonal process that teaches the infant that she is a human being. Without it, the baby remains a dishrag, as far as the mother is concerned, and the mother continues to feel like the dishrag's servant. The baby's response is not just a reward. It is a reflection of the mother's humanness, the response of one person to another. The sense of being a person in a special relationship — that of mother — grows throughout the symbiotic period.

81

2

Margaret Mahler and her coworkers, during their years of observation of infants which have contributed so much to our understanding of the psychological developments of earliest infancy, have also had a rare opportunity to observe mothers' behavior, since the babies were always seen with their mothers. Mahler has studied the personality differences in mothers that account for some of the differences in the ways that women react to motherhood.

Some mother-baby couples have what Mahler calls a "good fit," in which the baby and mother both settle easily into complementary roles at any particular stage in their development. Others are not so fortunate and appear to be out of phase at least some of the time. Mahler generally ascribes the problem to the mother's inability to mesh with the baby's needs and respond appropriately, and she gives little weight to the baby's inborn characteristics.

Films made in Mahler's experimental nursery show couples who have a "poor fit." One mother, for example, holds her three-month-old baby upright and facing away from her during feeding, denying the baby the cuddling and molding of one body to another that Mahler believes babies need. Another mother tries to control every interaction with her baby: She always leads the conversation. She tries to continue a game that the baby is trying to end and generally endeavors to be the one who establishes the rhythm of their relationship. Mahler may be right about these particular mothers. Their behavior with their babies may express their own inner conflict; but there are, of course, babies who won't cuddle down and mold to their mothers' bodies, or who simply don't like to be fed while in a recumbent position, even at this very early age. Some mothers, too, unconsciously or consciously recognize that their babies need more stimulation than most in order to become alert and playful. Behavior that is entirely appropriate with such a baby might be overstimulation for another baby. Brazelton, in *Infants and Mothers: Differences in Development*, describes these kinds of differences among babies and the ways in which adults' responses to them must be varied.

Mahler believes that the symbiotic relationship — the sense of oneness with the mother — is crucial to the child's later ability to separate and mature normally. She believes that a really bad "fit" can prevent normal psychological development in the baby, who is deprived of the feedback she needs in this crucial period. But even when the personalities of mother and baby don't mesh perfectly, the fit is rarely so bad as to cause the infant permanent damage. As Mahler discovered, when the situation approaches the danger point the infant herself may take steps to rectify the situation and get what she needs. The baby may, for instance, not emerge from the symbiotic phase until somewhat later than average, to get, over a longer time, the holding, cuddling, and mirroring that she needs. She may also embark on the next stage a month or so earlier than most, to free herself from being engulfed.

It is in these cases, the ones where the fit at a given stage is less than perfect, that having other caretakers makes life considerably easier for the baby, as well as for the mother. The baby who might otherwise have to prolong the symbiotic phase to get the emotional fueling required to enter the next phase of her emotional development may be able to get it from those who, unlike her mother, enjoy babies at their youngest and are able to provide what they need. A mother may be relieved of the burden of sole responsibility for a baby with whom she is not, at that moment, in tune.

Some of the differences in mothering, which begin to manifest themselves at this very early stage, may be the result of differences in the mothers' own early experiences. As Benedek has pointed out, a woman's unconscious holds a memory of her own symbiotic relationship with her mother, and that memory must serve to some extent to shape her maternal experience in symbiosis with her own infant. Freud has called this period of infancy "the unrememberable and the unforgettable." He believed, as most of us do, that the experience of infancy is preserved in the unconscious.

Every mother has had the experience (although usually when the child is somewhat older than those we are considering here) of finding herself doing or saying something exactly as her own mother did. It may be a tone of voice, an expression, a gesture; often it is something that was forgotten until the memory was activated by the mother's unpremeditated response to something her child did. Very often these incidents occur at times of high emotional charge — in situations of anger, pain, anxiety, stress, or great tenderness. It may be that a mother's unconscious, preverbal memory of infancy permits her empathy with her own baby, and by extension also accounts for the continuity in family patterns of parenting. If a mother's memory holds love and warmth and satisfaction, then that memory may impel her to recreate that infantile bliss for her own baby. And if the mother's memory holds too much frustration, according to Benedek, she may be unable to mother her own baby adequately.

Mothers have very different responses to the closeness of the symbiotic phase. Brett was a successful professional woman from a wealthy background who described this period as "the happiest time of my life." She had spent the last weeks of her pregnancy in bed because of a threatened premature delivery and was finally delivered by Caesarean section after twelve hours of labor. While every woman suffers some anxiety during pregnancy, there are some pregnancies, like Brett's, in which the woman may be even more anxious, and for good reason. If there has been a previous miscarriage, stillbirth, or neonatal death, if there is a threat of premature delivery, concern about the mother's own health or ability to withstand delivery, or if there is reason for concern about the baby's health, the anxiety may become all but paralyzing. But if the outcome of the delivery is good, the anxiety may be replaced by euphoria that may persist for several months. A woman who is euphoric does not escape the necessity for adjusting to motherhood, of course, but its trials may seem not as trying and its rewards may seem all the more delightful. Euphoria doesn't last forever, but while it does it can enhance the budding mother-infant relationship, just as depression can interfere with it.

Brett had suffered terrible anxiety in the last weeks of her pregnancy. The Caesarean, instead of being the bitter disappointment it so often is, brought relief; the miserable pregnancy was finally over. Ecstasy followed. At three months, Brett reported:

> ⤿ This has turned out to be the happiest time of my life. Chipper just has to smile and coo, and I feel great, no matter what calamity may have befallen me. The baby seems so important to me that all other worries and problems fade into the background. I feel very energetic and generally euphoric.

Brett's problems and calamities were neither serious nor usually terribly urgent. The housework, most of the cooking, and any routine baby care that Brett herself did not care to do were managed by others, even after her mother and the hired nurse left. By the time the baby was three months old, a trusted sitter came two afternoons and two evenings a week, so that Brett could go out with her husband or with friends.

As with many of the women I interviewed who were particularly competent and successful at their careers, the ease with which Brett slipped into mothering came as a real surprise to her:

> ⤿ Parenthood has brought out some qualities in my personality that I never knew existed. I seem to have some patience, much more tenderness, and an ability to relax and let things take their course without going into a tizzy. I tend to be an organized person, but the fact that I can't be very

organized with the baby's unpredictable schedule hasn't really bothered me.

Her husband, though he worked every day, shared her delight in the baby:

> ~ My husband is a model father — does all the diapering in the evenings and on weekends, takes the baby out for car rides and pram rides or entertains him while I'm out, squeezes in a few moments between the office and a business dinner just to catch a glimpse of the baby and me. He's very interested in the baby, just dotes on him.

Household help, the delight of both sets of grandparents with their new grandson, a cooperative and financially successful husband, and a happy, healthy baby all contributed to Brett's unusually untroubled start on motherhood, and she was willing to let it last:

> ~ I thought I would start free-lance work within a month of when the baby was born, but now I think I'll wait until early next year. I've learned that there's no point in predicting what I'll do, since I'm constantly changing my mind. I may return to full-time work in a few years, but it depends on what's available that would be interesting — not just a job for the sake of working — and on whether I've discovered any new interests between now and then which I'd rather pursue.

Brett's confidence in her ability to manage her own life and to continue to enjoy the baby was rooted, at least in part, in the comfort of her circumstances. Conditions were ideal for symbiosis, and Brett and the baby both seemed to revel in it:

> ~ Chipper is primarily interested in responding to people. He does a lot of smiling, cooing, kicking, thumbsucking, gurgling. He enjoys watching a musical mobile over his crib, loves to play on the changing table, likes to play with his hands, is captivated by someone talking to

him, watches me from his infant seat while I'm doing things around the kitchen or in the library. He responds best to the people he knows best — me, his father, and his baby-sitter — but he'll smile and make noises for anyone who pays attention to him. He rarely cries except if he's over-tired or ravenously hungry.

Beneath Brett's euphoria lies the characteristic pattern of the symbiotic phase: Chipper, in typical baby ways, draws his moth-er's attention. She responds, and in responding, grows more familiar with him, more comprehending of his ways of com-municating, and more comfortable in the relationship.

✎ I can't believe how happy I am. I just love looking at him and talking to him, and I love all the little sounds he makes and the way he smiles. He responds to *me* so much. It just goes on and on.

Not every mother hopes this stage will never end. For many women, the symbiotic phase is oppressive, stifling. The loss of an independent adult identity into the mothering role is not so easily accepted. She may feel that she is drowning, that she will never get out from under this relationship.

Sarah was one of several women I interviewed who experi-enced the dark side of symbiosis. She was twenty-seven and had put her husband, Peter, through law school before begin-ning graduate school herself. She planned to combine two or three children with a career in psychology. Jacob, her first, was three months old.

✎ I feel like a prisoner, trapped, with no way out. I feel like I'm in it with this kid for the next twenty years, like my life has to revolve around him. All my energy goes into him. I don't seem to have anything left for myself.

Work for many women is an essential part of their self-definition, and work is inevitably disrupted by the arrival of a baby. For Sarah, as for many of the women who stayed home with their babies, becoming a mother seemed to threaten her sense of self.

I'm starting to question for the first time whether I'm really going to be able to go back to school and get my Ph.D., and even if I did, what would I do then? Will I even be able to teach or anything? I just don't have any confidence in myself at all. I'm afraid that somewhere deep down I've always felt that a woman can only be a mother *or* have a career, but not both. There's no time for all that. My mother gave up her chance for having a career to have children.

An established free-lance designer, or a teacher with good maternity benefits and a guarantee of her old job, could slip into symbiosis confident that her life would not forever center on the baby. A woman like Brett, brought up in privileged circumstances, could let things take their course, confident that she would always find satisfactory solutions to any dilemma. (Nor did Brett spend the kind of time with her baby that Sarah did. Brett had help and was able to leave the house regularly. Sarah had none.) For many like Sarah, looking forward to having to create their own solutions to the baby-career dilemma, symbiosis was frightening. They began to fear the future, as they became more and more deeply submerged in mothering, losing confidence in their own ability to control their lives, to find time for themselves, even to think.

Jacob's life is certainly more important, but I need something for myself, too. Sometimes I feel like there's no point in going on. This is what my life is going to be: taking care of him, doing things with him.

Her expectations of motherhood had been rather different from the reality:

People would tell me, "You're not going to have time to read or anything." I really love to read, and I said, "Oh, I'm going to have plenty of time to read." I'd heard that some babies sleep twenty hours a day. I had no idea. Sometimes I read for a few minutes while I'm breastfeeding. I've read about a third of a novel since he was born.

Sarah, as you may have gathered, was somewhat depressed. I was surprised, then, when Jacob woke from his nap, and she brought him into the kitchen where we had been talking, to see that her expression had changed completely. She was animated, smiling and talking to the baby. When we resumed the interview, she said:

✧ There are so many things about him that I love. It's so amazing to me, to see all the things that he's learning. Just yesterday, I gave him a rattle, and he reached for it, and then he handed it from one hand to the other. Then he dropped it in his lap and picked it up. All at once. I couldn't believe it. It was just so exciting. I kept making him do it over and over.

The symbiotic oneness, its warmth and satisfaction, should be blissful for the infant. It need not be so for the mother. For the mother, the heart of the matter is not bliss, but closeness — the empathy and the indelible bond that she begins to feel for her child. Some women thrive on the symbiotic relationship; others chafe in it. For Sarah, happiness did not come as it did for Brett, if the baby would only smile and coo. She needed more from him — needed to see him developing — and her interest in him and attachment to him increased as he grew and learned to do new things.

3

By the time the baby is two or three or four months old, many mothers have gone back to outside jobs. Those who do often suffer. Ellen, whose son Daniel was born on the first page of this book, returned to her job part-time when Daniel was two months old. A few weeks later, she said:

❧ I really feel the world's judgment about going back to work. For a while, when I told people I was working, I would minimize the time I spent out of the house. I said I was working ten hours a week, when I was really working sixteen. If I told them an hour more, I was afraid they'd be more disapproving. It's going against the cultural grain, and I feel that very intensely.

It is clear that babies at this stage need a great deal of nurturance, social interchange, and play, in addition to simple physical care, if they are to develop properly. It is much less clear that all this, which we call "mothering," must be care given by the mother.

The notion that no one but the mother can mother is very much in fashion today, but it is a fairly recent idea. Even in the nineteenth century, when motherhood was glorified, middle-class mothers (who were the ones being glorified, after all) had nurses and nannies, governesses and tutors who did most of the work of what we call mothering. It was after World War II, as Ann Dally points out in *Inventing Motherhood*, that the idea was first raised that an exclusive relationship with the mother was necessary for a child's mental health.

John Bowlby, the British psychoanalyst, wrote a report for the World Health Organization in the early 1950s. In it he said:

> What is believed to be essential for mental health is that the infant and young child should experience a warm, intimate, and continuous relationship with his mother (or permanent mother-substitute) in which both find satisfaction and enjoyment. . . . A state of affairs in which the child does not have this relationship is termed "maternal deprivation."

Bowlby based his opinion on a number of studies of children in orphanages, hospitals, and other institutions, and of children separated from their parents by the war. These children had suffered multiple traumas, being separated from their parents and their homes, being cared for by a succession of overworked nurses on changing shifts, suffering illness and (in the cases of the children in orphanages) neglect and extreme sensory deprivation. The institutionalized children were kept in cribs or beds, were rarely spoken to, and had no toys and no one to play with. All the children Bowlby studied had difficulty forming attachments to others. The institutionalized children were developmentally retarded, as well.

Even a short separation had its effect on a child. Bowlby quotes descriptions of children in hospitals where visits from parents were not permitted, who would cry in protest for a time, then sink into a listless, detached state. When returned to their mothers they were, at least for a time, tense and insecure. They clung to their mothers and had difficulty sleeping.

It is from this evidence that Bowlby drew his conclusion that any separation from mother constituted "maternal deprivation" and would be harmful to the child. His position should not be underestimated. He believes that babies can attach to only one primary figure and that that primary figure — the mother or permanent mother-substitute — must *always* be available:

> The provision of constant attention day and night, seven days a week and 365 in the year, is possible only for a woman who derives profound satisfaction from seeing her child grow from babyhood, through the many phases of childhood, to become an independent man or woman, and knows that it is her care which has made this possible.

While Bowlby acknowledges that not every mother is a good mother — that some are cold or hostile or neglectful — his standard of adequate mothering takes into account only the continuity of the relationship, and not its quality. Numerous explanations have been advanced as to why Bowlby's work, which was soon popularized in England and then in the United States, became so widely accepted. Certainly, it fit in nicely with the drive to return women to the home after World War II and the feminine mystique of the 50s. Dally points out, too, that the idealization of the mother implicit in Bowlby's theory was likely to appeal to the generation of Englishwomen raised by nannies and newly deprived of servants of their own. These women, whose mothers were often distant and glamorous figures, were likely to have idealized their mothers and to feel the need to become that idealized mother. (Dally also remarks that Bowlby himself, a member of the British upper class, is likely to suffer from idealization of the mother.)

More recently, the quality of the time that a mother spends with her child has received more attention. Margaret Mahler, the psychoanalyst who is author of *The Psychological Birth of the Human Infant*, also believes that mother is necessary. But all her time alone is not enough. If the mother "is unpredictable, unstable, anxiety-ridden or hostile, if her confidence in herself as a mother is shaky, then the individuating child has to do without a reliable frame of reference for checking back, perceptually and emotionally, to the symbiotic partner." More recently, the developmental psychologist Selma Fraiberg, in *Every Child's Birthright*, has argued that any "rupture of human ties in infancy . . . can produce certain disturbances in the later functioning of the child and can impair to varying degrees the capacity of the child to bind himself to human partners later in childhood."

All these demands for perfection, and the consequences of imperfection, were on the minds of most of the mothers I interviewed a good part of the time. Mothers who work outside their homes or who continue their schooling are often made to feel selfish and guilty of neglect. Today every mother seems aware that it is considered ideal for her to stay home and take care of her baby "day and night, seven days a week and 365 in the year." (How long she is required to do so varies with the expert being quoted. The range is one month to six years.) Any mother who doesn't stay home, or who fears that she doesn't always respond promptly to meet all the baby's needs, who sometimes feels anxious or hostile or lacking in confidence, worries at some point about not being a "good mother," and since we rest on the mother so much of the responsibility for producing a well-behaved, successful, well-adjusted, affectionate, responsible child, mothers have plenty to worry about.

While the children that Bowlby studied were unquestionably damaged by their experience of deprivation, it takes a considerable leap of the imagination to equate them with children who are cared for by their mothers *and* their fathers and their babysitters or the workers in a day-care center. Nonetheless, this very leap has caused the guilt that mothers feel when they leave their babies. They worry that their absence will prevent the baby from loving them, and that it will somehow affect the baby's later development.

The fact is that no one has demonstrated *any* actual benefit to a baby of having only one caretaker. Babies do need consistency; they need some limited, stable, familiar group of people to care for them. Studies in the United States and abroad have shown few differences in emotional, social, or physical development between children raised at home and those who spend most of their waking time in well-run day-care centers, and the differences that have been found are small. Depending on which study you read, day-care children may be slightly more physically active, aggressive, peer-oriented, or comfortable in unfamiliar situations. (The point, often made, that most day-care centers fall far short of those where these studies have been done is no argument against day care for babies. That argument does, however, support a call for increased funding and greater public and governmental concern.)

There is also no evidence that babies in day care do not have special attachments to their mothers. Jerome Kagan, a developmental psychologist at Harvard, has compared children who were in a day-care center five days a week from the age of three and a half months with a matched group of home-raised children and found that the two groups showed no differences in attachment to their mothers. Even children in Israeli kibbutzes, who are raised in group nurseries with one primary caretaker and visit their parents only a few hours a day, show a specific attachment for their mothers. "It is not clear," writes Kagan, "why this is so."

Daniel's first two months were, for Ellen, difficult and anxious ones. She hated the sound of his crying, couldn't adjust to his inability to stay on a schedule, and felt exhausted, out of control, and miserable. At two months, finding a sitter and making the necessary arrangements to return to work seemed to Ellen like the last straw:

> ~ I'm completely overwhelmed. I can't seem to figure out what would be the best hours for me to work, in terms of his schedule, or what days, in terms of what has to be done at work. I can't always figure out when to tell people to come for interviews. I put an ad in the paper, so people call, and I don't know what to ask them, or what I'm looking for, or anything. And then, should I ask them to come over when he's probably going to be asleep, so I can talk to them without being interrupted, or should I have them come when he's awake, so I can see how they handle him and how he reacts to them? And does the way they are with him when I'm here bear any relation to the way they'll be when I'm not? I just don't know. What I do know is I can't handle this.

She eventually did, of course. Ellen found a responsible woman who loved little babies, and she figured out a reasonable work schedule for herself. In spite of all her misgivings, she adjusted quickly to the new routine and found that she enjoyed the time away from Daniel and that spending a limited amount of time with him was far more rewarding than spending all her time with him had been.

> ~ I work four mornings a week now. When I get home, he's usually napping — it's funny how Dee got him on a schedule so fast — so I get a chance to talk to her about

how things went that day. When he gets up, we play, I nurse him, we sometimes go out. I feel really relaxed with him now. I feel like the time I'm with him is *his* time. I think that before, when I was home all the time, I always felt divided — like I was with him, but I really should be doing something else, cooking dinner maybe, or the laundry. It's weird, because I really didn't have that much else to do. I always felt, when I was with Danny, that I wasn't really doing anything and that I should be doing *something*. I guess now that my work is the something, I don't feel so guilty about just playing with him for an hour. It revives me.

I asked Ellen how she felt about work:

～ The first few days were very difficult. I worried about him, about how he was going to take it. I was afraid that he'd forget who I was. It was hard to remember what I was supposed to be doing at the office. But since the first week, we've both been doing very well. I work very concentratedly while I'm there, and he gets so excited when he sees me that it's clear he knows that I'm his Mommy.

Judith was another professional woman who returned to her job when her three-month maternity leave was up. She had enjoyed being home for the last month and dreaded the return to work. After she had been back at work for a month, she told me:

～ I thought it would get easier, but it hasn't. I think about Susannah all the time while I'm working. I feel guilty about leaving her, even though I know she's in good hands and she's happy when I leave and happy when I get home. I just feel like I leave a part of myself at home when I go to work.

There could scarcely be a clearer statement of a mother's symbiotic attachment to her child: "I feel like I leave a part of myself at home." Why then did Ellen, who seemed to love Daniel as

95

much as Judith did Susannah, *not* feel torn by leaving him? If Ellen had loved her job and Judith hated hers, the difference might have been understandable, but both had work that they liked.

Another mother, who felt depressed and frustrated while at home with the baby, decided that a job was the solution. It was, but only in part. She was much relieved to be out of the house, but continued to feel guilty about the baby. She started working when the baby was about three-and-a-half months old, and after two months of full-time work she said:

> ◯ I'm constantly torn. I feel like I should be home with her, like going back to work was a cop-out. I try to convince myself that she's better off this way, but I feel like I ran away from some very important task I was supposed to do. I feel like I should've stuck it out, no matter how awful it was for me or for her.

After several other interviews with women who went back to work within the first three or four months of the baby's life, I realized that for most of them a return *before* the symbiotic pattern was established was less likely to create conflict for the mother than would a return a month or so later. The reason, I believe, is that if the relationship with the infant is established from the beginning as a part-time thing, then mother and baby both seem to be able to adjust to it with a fair amount of ease. It is when the relationship, once established, is significantly altered by being shifted from full-time to part-time that the mother, at least, seems to have more difficulty coping. The period from six to eight weeks, a natural transition point in the relationship, is one of several times that changes in the relationship are easier to accomplish.

4

Mothers in the symbiotic phase tend to be more interested in their babies than they are in anything else. This seems to hold as true for those with outside work as it does for those who are at home all day, and as true for those who are feeling burdened and beset as for those who are perfectly delighted with every aspect of their new role. Because they are so acutely concerned with the baby, mothers in this phase often feel most comfortable with mothers of other infants, so that when they do begin to go out, they seek out other mothers. I have watched them, been among them as they sort themselves into cohorts according to the ages of their babies on warm afternoons in the park — mothers of babies three months old on one group of benches; mothers of babies just a little younger or older on others.

The babies are discussed endlessly, with the most minute attention paid to every detail of habit or development. One of the reasons, of course, that mothers must discuss these things with other mothers is that people without babies (or without some compelling professional interest in them) are notoriously intolerant of these discussions. Even the mothers themselves sometimes feel a bit foolish discussing the minutiae of burping. A certain amount of bragging and competition is evident in these conversations, but something else is going on as well. As one mother put it:

> ✍ I feel like my brains have turned to pudding and that my fascination with how much he eats or how often he spits it up is probably a prime symptom of my mental deterioration, but it helps me to see other mothers going through the same thing, so I know that at least I'm not the only one who's like this.

Being able to use the other mothers as a mirror not only helps a mother feel less crazy, but validates her experience, making it more real and easier to understand.

Women seek out other mothers not only to find reflections of themselves, but also for simple adult companionship. They fear isolation. The things that can happen to mothers when they are left too long alone with their babies are the stuff of nightmares and shocked rumors. The fantasies that were told to me by stable, easygoing women — holding the baby over the gas flame, hurling the baby against the wall — were terrifying. Symbiosis between mother and infant is not a pathological state, remember. The mother's ego — her self — is not completely absorbed into the symbiotic relationship. At those times when she feels herself becoming completely submerged in the relationship, when her defenses are reduced by exhaustion or boredom or an overwhelming need for someone to talk to, mothers often rebel with thoughts of destroying the baby. While the fantasies do serve to let off steam, for many women they engender guilt and often depression.

Sarah was a woman who had almost no one to talk to. She lived a thousand miles from her family and had moved to a new and unfamiliar neighborhood when Jacob was just a month old. A long spell of bitterly cold weather had kept her in the house at one point for nine days running. On the evening of the ninth day, her husband called at six o'clock, the very hour he was due home, to say that he would be delayed another hour or two. The baby, like many his age, had a regular fussy period that usually began around five in the afternoon. Often his father's arrival could distract him and restore him to his usual, more cheerful self. On this particular evening, Jacob would not be calmed by his mother. By seven o'clock, she had thrown him into his crib and had begun slamming the crib, with the baby in it, again and again against the nursery wall.

꙳ I must've done it four or five times, hard, and then I sort of "came to" and realized what I was doing. I was so scared. I thought I might've hurt Jake. Fortunately, he was OK. I picked him up and sat and rocked with him and cried and cried. He was very quiet. He seemed sort of surprised.

By the time Peter got home, it was all over, and when I told him what had happened, I could tell he thought I was making it up just to make him feel guilty for being late.

It was Sarah, not her husband, who felt guilty and frightened by the murderous rage that had overtaken her. She worried that it might mean she could not be trusted to be a good mother to Jacob. Nearly every woman I interviewed had a similar story to recount. Each one had at least one occasion when she lost control. Often it occurred at the end of the day; sometimes, as with Sarah, when expected relief was unexpectedly unavailable. Some of the mothers had struck the babies; some had shaken them. Some had screamed and most had cried. No one admitted to having hurt the baby, but babies frequently are injured by their mothers, as hospital and police statistics prove.

The mothers all counted this loss of control as a personal failure, a breakdown of their perfect fit with their babies. A recent study conducted at the University of Wisconsin, however, concluded that "child abuse could just as easily be the product of situational stress as personal pathology. In other words, given the right circumstances, *anyone* might step over the line." The fact is that the line lies very close to where most mothers live. The needs of the infant are unending, and no woman, no matter how well constituted she may be to enter into a symbiotic relationship, can meet them all, day after day, without protest. Rachel, who was as contented in the symbiotic relationship as anyone I met, was the woman who thought about holding her baby over the flames. She told me that I was the only person to whom she had admitted that fantasy, which had disturbed her greatly.

Rachel, like many mothers of young babies, had only herself to rely on. Though her husband helped, he and Rachel both considered him to be helping with *her* job. The assumption that the baby's physical care and its emotional sustenance must always come from the mother contributes heavily to a mother's frustration at being unable to manage it all without a strain, to admit to herself or anyone else that she can't quite cope or to ask for help. The women who are most isolated in this period — those who have no nearby friends or family and whose husbands, as many do, have withdrawn emotionally after the baby's birth — often begin to focus more and more on the baby. They undertake not only to be the sole frame of reference for the infant's budding sense of self, but to get all their own emotional fueling from the infant. Their dual isolation and the growing exclusivity of their relationship provide a hothouse atmosphere for the transplantation and growth of all sorts of neuroses.

No matter how close she and her mother may be, however, the baby in these few months will begin to learn that there is a difference between things that arise from within herself and those that come to her from the world outside. She learns this difference by two mechanisms. The first and more positive is the social interaction between herself and her mother (and the others who care for her regularly). In these months of symbiosis, the most noticeable development is the expansion of the number and variety of interchanges between mother and baby. They smile at each other and converse and play in a more and more complex and reciprocal fashion. They mimic each other and engage in simple back-and-forth games. It is through these exchanges that the baby learns not only that she is separate, but that she is a person much like the one who imitates her sounds and gestures, who smiles back when she smiles, who (sometimes) comes when she is needed.

The second mechanism by which a baby comes to recognize her separateness entails a kind of negative feedback. Mothers are not perfect, and no mother, no matter how hard she tries, can fill all the baby's needs as soon as they are felt. The baby, therefore, from time to time feels frustrated. She begins to lose her sense of omnipotence, the sense that she is in control of having her needs met. If the baby were in control — if her mother were really a part of her — then she could not be frustrated as she is. So the baby gradually learns through frustration that someone else, someone separate from her, is really in control and can respond or not, apparently arbitrarily. While the baby will not experience herself as a fully separate being for a long time, before she is five months old she will begin to experience new physical drives, and these will usher in new social developments and the next stage in the emotional growth of infant and mother. But for now, even mothers who work outside or who have help at home are bound as tightly as they ever will be into the role of mother. Motherhood still dominates every part of their lives.

CHAPTER 4

THE FIFTH MONTH
Hatching

> The mother . . . is connected with this
> other being by the most mundane and
> the most invisible strands, in a way she
> can be connected with no one else ex-
> cept in the deep past of her own infant
> connection with her own mother. And
> she too needs to struggle from that one-
> to-one intensity into a new realization,
> or reaffirmation, of her being-unto-
> herself.
> — ADRIENNE RICH, *Of Woman Born*, p. 36

WHEN MOLLY was just past four months old, she and I went
to the shore for a needed vacation. (My husband was working
and joined us only on the weekends.) I had finished my first
book, working that few hours a week that Molly was at the
babysitter's, and had sent it off to the editor. We had a house
at the beach that we were sharing with friends for a month.
Molly was delightful, attentive to everything around her, learning to reach and grasp so that she could now play with toys,
enjoying new foods and the new perspective that she got from
being wheeled about in a stroller instead of a carriage. I had a
terrible time. I worried about the book and wondered if I'd ever
write another. I didn't want to be just a mother, but I didn't
know if I could be anything else. I was withdrawn and irritable
and spent most of my time reading. Taking care of Molly was
a relief. Her demands were limited and comprehensible, and

her familiar body and smile afforded me, I felt, a sanity-sustaining hold on reality. I was confident of my ability to mother her. I doubted my ability to do anything else as well, yet I knew that mothering alone was not enough for me.

Before the month was up, I abruptly returned to the city, brought my résumé up to date and determinedly began looking for a job. A search for work in New York during an August heat wave would not strike most people as an improvement over a vacation at the beach, but it got me out, moving, seeing people, thinking about my future in concrete terms, and before long my mind began to clear, my sense of humor improved, and my equanimity was restored. But all that took some time, and before my crisis was resolved I suffered and caused a good deal of pain.

From the middle of the second month to the fifth, most women don't think about themselves a great deal. In conversation the subject of the baby dominates, and the women rarely spontaneously say anything about themselves unless it has to do with the relationship to the baby. The core of a mother's attention is reserved for the baby and the emerging relationship with her. During the fifth month, however, there are a number of developments on the baby's part that rupture the symbiotic duality and eventually force the mother's attention back on herself. In the fifth month virtually every mother I interviewed offered some variant of the observation: "I don't know what's happened to me," or "I feel like I've forgotten who I am," or, as one mother put it, "I feel like I went somewhere and I'm not back yet."

The emergence from symbiosis — for that is what is going on here — is not easily accomplished by a mother, and it is quite often accompanied by a fair amount of emotional turmoil for the woman herself and often, too, for her family and friends. But emerge is what the mother must do, because the symbiotic tie to the infant must now begin to loosen. During this month and the next a mother must regain her sense of identity as an adult woman and begin to remember who she was before the baby, before she became a mother. She travels an unmarked route, especially so the first time. Some women don't fully accomplish the tasks of this month; most do. But because the task is so unfamiliar, most women begin it with no sense of what is to be done, no knowledge that there is a goal to be achieved or what that goal is. When the change begins, women often feel confused, disoriented, frustrated. Like the other stages in the development of a mother, this one is set off by developments in the baby.

When I went back to see Ellen, who had adjusted so well to her return to her job, I was struck first by the changes in Daniel, who was by this time five months old. Six weeks earlier he, like most babies, was happiest in a recumbent position while feeding. I arrived one afternoon shortly after Ellen had returned home from work. She was trying to nurse Daniel. A few weeks before, we had had a long and seldom interrupted interview under similar circumstances. Now, every time either of us began to speak, Daniel would drop the nipple and attend to whoever was talking. Several times, almost compulsively, he tried to get to his feet, or he would start vocalizing, obviously trying to join the conversation. It was funny. It was also impossible for us to talk or for Ellen to feed him. At last I volunteered to leave the room until the feeding was finished.

When Ellen and I resumed our conversation, Daniel spent most of his time standing on Ellen's lap while she held him under the armpits to help support his weight. He still took advantage of every pause in the conversation to try to join in, twisted himself around to see me every time I spoke, grabbed at Ellen's necklace and earrings, and made himself generally hard to ignore.

That supported standing posture is so characteristic of babies between four and five months that from the position alone it is possible to make a guess at the baby's age. At three months he lay cradled in his mother's arms, gazing into her eyes. Now he pushes to his feet, straightens his arms against his mother's chest, arches his back, and turns his gaze to the side, trying, it seems, to look behind him. Try as a mother may to hold her infant, to keep him cuddled in her lap, she finds that the infant will not be restrained, that something within the baby is driving him out of the symbiotic orbit and into the world. The mutuality, the comfortable holding of the past months is at an end; the first separation is at hand. The baby has begun to realize that he and his mother are not a single, unified being.

The symbiotic tie could best be seen in the infant's firm hold on the nipple and her unblinking gaze into her mother's eyes during feeding. Now both of these begin to loosen. She nurses eagerly for a minute or two; then, at some slight sound, she turns from the nipple. If someone has entered the room, the baby may reach out, smiling and vocalizing; she'd really rather play. Her behavior, almost sure to get a response, makes feeding her a more strenuous and time-consuming procedure for the mother, who must repeatedly return the baby's attention to the business of feeding.

The baby now looks around and reaches for objects, for people, for attention. To say that the baby had rejected her mother would be going too far, although some mothers do feel rejected. But the drive of the infant is irresistible, and there is little a mother can do but acquiesce to it. The infant has begun to hatch.

Babies at this age are extremely sociable, and while they recognize the differences between familiar people and strangers, most will smile and gurgle and reach out to anyone who pays attention to them. Though the baby cannot yet sit unsupported, she flips and wriggles when left to herself. She can propel herself right out of an infant seat and becomes more prone to accidents. This sudden burst of activity makes her seem fearless, ready to strike out on her own. The steady, loving gaze that was so recently the core of her tie to her mother no longer satisfies her. Her attention is now directed outward, to others, to the whole world around her.

In the fifth month the interactions between infants and others become more complicated and extensive. A baby recognizes her name and will often respond to it with attention and vocalizing, even when it occurs in the course of others' conversation. Her demands are more complex. She no longer simply wants attention; she may want the attention of a particular person, or she may want to play a particular game. She reaches for things, if she is sitting, and can smoothly grasp whatever is within reach. She knows enough to search for an object where she left it and to follow the path of a falling toy that she has dropped. Just cooing at her will no longer keep her amused. She wants to hand a toy back and forth or drop a rattle and have her mother pick it up.

All these developments, of course, can leave a mother feeling that she no longer quite understands what to do or what the baby wants or needs. Many women interpret the developments as new demands on them, as Brenda did:

> ∿ She's becoming a person. You say to yourself: "You can't just leave the kid in the crib. If you're not going to talk to her and play with her, she's not going to develop right." It does affect them. You can't ignore them or it affects their personality. They're not going to have the same IQ or emotional development.

Having dozens of ways to play with the baby might be assumed to enhance the relationship between a woman and her infant. If that relationship proceeded on a linear course, it would simply be enriched by each of the baby's new skills, which would increase the number of ways in which the partners could interact. But in the fifth month mothers begin to understand that as the baby grows and develops her very growth implies the end of infancy and dependency. The actual end of infancy, of course, is some months away, and dependency is a lifelong characteristic of human relationship.

These mothers are not just having paranoid fancies about their babies growing up and abandoning them. The fifth month does in fact represent the first of the many steps toward independence that the child will eventually take. And mothers know this, even if they are not consciously aware of it, even when they can't articulate exactly what is happening or how it makes them feel. When Brenda (who did not regret the development at all) said, "She's becoming a person," we are already hearing a woman mourn the passing of something precious and transitory: the earliest and most helpless part of infancy.

Many women — those with absorbing careers or those who are simply not comfortable with helpless infants — could be assumed to welcome the new developments, but while many women are pleased to see the signs of maturity that their babies show in the fifth month, no one seems to greet them with entirely unmixed feelings. The baby's motor drives and her developing skills, her widening field of interest and her sociability, evoke different responses from different mothers. The mother who enjoyed the symbiotic state may feel abandoned. The mother who hated it generally feels relief, though her relief is often mixed with guilt, as though she were being punished for rejecting the baby. The woman who appreciates and encourages every sign of the baby's independence must still cope with what that independence will mean to her life. While it may be welcome, the baby's turning away poses a threat to her mother: The solutions and adjustments that have sufficed up to now will not any longer. For every mother, the fifth month is a time for reappraisal.

As the babies break the intense mutual gaze and begin to look elsewhere, their mothers seem agitated, restless, and discontented. Even those who have long since returned to outside work or other activities find that the particular kind of attention they had focused so intently on their babies is no longer required. The baby has decided that the world is full of things at least as interesting as Mom. And so Mom is suddenly thrown back on her own resources. She has no motor drives, no developmental imperatives to push her into a new relationship to herself, or to the baby or the world. She needs something new to pay attention to, and the first and most obvious object is herself, nearly forgotten in the intensity of her duality with the infant. She looks at the baby and she seems to ask, "Where have *I* been all your life?"

While she has been absorbed by motherhood for only a few months, that absorption has been profound. She needs first to remember who she was before she became a mother, but before she can recall that, or put the memories to use, there is a time when everything seems terribly difficult. The baby and the baby's needs seem to fill her day, but without the satisfaction they gave a few weeks earlier. For many women, what occurs is an identity crisis, necessary but painful.

Chipper's mother, whose life was made so much easier than most by a housekeeper and regular sitter, at three months had said: "The baby just has to smile and coo, and I feel great no matter what calamity may have befallen me." At five months, she had a sadder tune. The ideal babysitter had turned out not to be so wonderful and had to be let go. The little routines of child care were no longer so attractive; in fact, she could hardly bear to talk about them. She began to lose confidence in herself, but was fortunate to get some free-lance work to keep herself busy:

> ~ I have lots of doubts about whether or not I can do a good job and still give my time without resentment to Chipper and to my husband and still have time for other things. While this work renews some feeling of self-respect, it forces me to stay at home during the day to cram in as much work as possible while Chipper sleeps. Of course, I'm desperate for conversation when my husband gets home, and I want to pour out my frustrations to him. On weekends I'm dying to do something exciting. My husband is willing to do anything I feel like doing, but I know he would prefer to relax at home with his son.
>
> In this period of uncertainty, when I'm facing entirely new situations and where each need I have conflicts with

another — the free-lance work which helps my ego keeps me in the house away from the adult companionship I so desperately need — I am almost incapacitated by indecision. What kind of daytime help do I need? Pick-up sitters? Regular help one or two days a week? What will I do? Where will I go? How will I use my free time out in the world? Should I get involved in some significant civic work? Should I go back to my old employer for part-time work, to get trapped in the problems I wanted to get away from? Should I look for other part-time work? Should I find the help first and then the outside activity, or the other way around? I can't answer any of these questions. Because I lack confidence in this completely new role with its new identity, I'm terrified of committing myself to anything else that's new. What if I get involved in something else and then feel guilty about the baby, or find the outside activity unsatisfying and not worth the sacrifice?

If Brett's confusion was generalized, Lillian's was quite specific. Lillian, a professor of linguistics, had taught for more than fifteen years before taking a few months off to have her first baby. She was euphoric during the first months; her daughter meant the world to her. She had been a competent and popular teacher, respected by her colleagues. She returned to her job when Anna was three months old, but by the time Anna reached five months, Lillian found herself paralyzed by anxiety:

⌣⌢ I was afraid to go to school. I was terrified of teaching. It got so bad that I went into therapy because I was afraid that I just couldn't do it any more. You have to understand I had been doing this — teaching — for years. It should've been second nature. The surface content was that I had no time to prepare my classes, but underneath I couldn't see myself as a teacher. It was as if that part of me had disappeared.

We might assume that a woman who had no role conflicts would not suffer the kind of crisis that afflicts the woman who is trying to balance motherhood with a career or a job. For the woman who intends to stay at home as a full-time mother, the path should be smoother. She has become what she set out to be, and there seems less likelihood of discontent. Such is not the case. The mothers who had no outside work on which to express their sense of frustration focused it on mothering.

Joanne was twenty, and Jennifer was her first child. Joanne had held a secretarial job from the time she graduated from high school until the sixth month of her pregnancy. She didn't especially like her job. She and her husband agreed that she should stay at home until all their children were of school age, and by her husband's putting in some overtime, they could manage without Joanne's paycheck. She kept a neat house and a clean baby. By the time Jennifer was five months old, she had been on a schedule, which included sleeping through the night, for several months. Her routine, at this time, included a daily outing. Joanne said to me:

> ~ I think I'm going to stop going to the playground. Obviously, I don't go for her sake, since she can't even sit up yet. We go almost every afternoon, and the babies sleep in their carriages, and what do we talk about? We talk about what goes into the babies and what comes out of the babies and how often and what it looks like. I can't stand it any more. I'll just have to find something else to do.

Joanne began looking for that "something else," as many mothers do, by reaching into the recent past:

> ~ I called a friend, a girl I used to work with. I really wanted to talk to someone. But *I* had nothing to say. She doesn't have any kids, so she's not that interested in the baby, and there's nothing to tell anyone about my life. She told me all the office gossip, and that was great, except that afterwards I felt like I'd been down a hole for the past five months and life had passed me by.

The crisis of the fifth month was perhaps best summed up by Brenda:

∿ All of a sudden, you just get to the point where you say, "Gee, I'm coping very nicely with the whole thing. I have a baby and I have my life, and I'm doing just fine." And then you suddenly realize: I'm not doing *anything*. The house is a mess, you're screaming at the kids and yelling at the dog.

It was in the fifth-month interviews that many women began to mention their husbands. Before that, if he was mentioned at all, the mention had to do with his willingness to "help out," or his acceptance of the baby. Now he seemed to have returned to his wife's consciousness *as a husband*. Many husbands were beginning to insist that their wives act more like wives. Many of them were genuinely helpful and involved with the babies; some were not. Most men, by five months, were beginning to insist that life return to normal, at least as far as the marriage was concerned. Their sleep, too, had often been interrupted. Many husbands were doing night feedings or getting up to bring the baby to a nursing mother. Most felt that they had been demoted to a distant second place during their wives' immersion in symbiosis, and many resented that. For many couples the greatest conflict centered around the issue of sexual relations.

That new mothers are not interested in sex is a well-known but seldom discussed fact. When a woman goes to her obstetrician for the six-week postpartum checkup, the doctor invariably tells her that she can resume sexual relations. Aside from a discussion of birth control, there is rarely any further mention of the matter. The common experience among the women I interviewed was that they had attempted intercourse and immediately concluded that there was something wrong — with themselves. Ellen's response was typical:

∿ We tried it and it hurt. In fact, it was agonizing. I told the doctor about it, and he said, "Everything is fine.

There's no reason you should be sore.'' I felt like he was telling me I was frigid.

Much later, another woman said:

～ I was so tight and so dry, and it kept hurting, and then I'd anticipate that it was going to hurt and get more tense. It went on like that for almost a year.

For most women the first problem was the episiotomy. The modern obstetrician's proclivity for reducing the size of a grown woman's vagina to that of a seven-year-old's (claiming that it will improve sex — for her husband) sometimes seems to border on the sadistic. There were few women for whom intercourse was not painful for a few weeks, and many felt discomfort for months. For the women who were breastfeeding, vaginal lubrication seldom returned to normal before the baby was fully weaned. When a baby is up once or more every night demanding attention, fatigue is certainly a factor in the mother's lack of sexual desire. Still, as Joanne said, referring to her sex life before the baby: "If you weren't in the mood, you'd get in the mood. If you were too tired, you'd get *un*tired.''

The real sexual problem — the utter absence of interest and desire — cannot be completely explained by the physical factors. First, it seems to outlast the physical problems; second, it seems so deep and pervasive; third, every one of the eight adoptive mothers I interviewed also reported a lack of sex drive. While several of the adoptive mothers attributed their lack of sexual interest to fatigue, it seemed, on further questioning, that this fatigue had not interfered as seriously with any other aspect of their lives. Many of the women, of course, found breastfeeding to be sexually arousing. But that arousal did not seem to be translated into adult sexual desire, and when I asked the women if they had sexual fantasies that accompanied that sexual excitement, everyone said no. The giving and getting between mother and infant, while unquestionably sensual, seemed to remain on the infant's level. By five months, many of the husbands felt sorely deprived, the women felt guilty, and in many of the marriages the problems were becoming acute.

Motherhood and sexuality have traditionally been viewed as mutually exclusive, or at least as largely incompatible. The distinction between good girl and bad girl or the Madonna and the whore is one that most women in our culture have internalized from a fairly early age. Many women feel that dichotomy directly: Becoming a mother not only *changes* your sexuality, it is *supposed* to change your sexuality. Joanne made this comment:

> ✎⁀ I walk down the street, and I look very nice, and if a man says anything to me or makes a comment about how I look, I think, well, he doesn't know I'm a mother.

The Freudian theorists who have examined the question, especially Helene Deutsch and Marie Bonaparte, believe that "mature" sexuality in a woman (reproductively directed and therefore maternal) is passive and receptive, lacking the drive which is the characteristic of male sexuality. A "masculine," active sex drive in a woman, they believe, is found in a woman who is immature and who fears or rejects motherhood. Sexual feelings and maternal feelings, for the Freudians, do not coexist. This sorry conclusion seems to have been accepted by a good many women, including writers such as Nancy Friday, who believes that mothers inevitably suppress their daughters' sexuality so that the daughters will themselves become mothers and not free women.

Mothering has its own sexual content, in the sexual arousal of breast feeding, in the identification with the infant's visible pleasure in her mother's caring for her and in her discovery of her own body, in the mother's delight in the sensuousness of her infant's body. Adrienne Rich presents a poetic and powerful vision of the possibility of reclaiming maternity, not "as a kind of production, but as part of female experience . . . enmeshed with sexuality, with the ebb and flow of . . . sexual desire," unfettered by the proscriptions and constraints of patriarchal society.

The fact is that mothers — *new* mothers — don't feel very sexy, in the adult sense. And their lack of desire seems to go deeper than the simple notion that, "Mother doesn't do those things and now that I am a mother, neither do I." Sexuality, the kind we all strive for is described by active concepts: sexual drive, sexual desire. It requires, at its best, a mutual surrender of selves.

A sense of self, a sense of identity implies a sense of continuity with the past. But it is exactly that sense of continuous self (which Erik Erikson calls the "ego identity") that is lost in the experience of childbirth and early motherhood. The mother's sense of self, both her psychic sense and her physical integrity, are shattered in childbirth and early motherhood, which requires a total surrender of the self to an irreversible process. Giving birth is an experience of extreme pain and often of fear, an overwhelming violation of our everyday experience of ourselves. The sense of wonder at the baby, so recently inside, now mysteriously outside, and its companion sense of retained connectedness to her all imply a disturbed (but not abnormal) sense of psychic and physical integrity and separateness. Sarah was one of many women who reported similar feelings:

> ╰╮ When we try to make love, I find I can't get into it. I keep thinking about Jacob, wondering if he's going to wake up and hear us, because he sleeps near us. Or I worry that I'll just start to really get into it and then he's going to start to cry. Or I imagine I hear him crying.

Rachel told a startling and illuminating story:

> ╰╮ I hadn't been able to have an orgasm at all. Then, just recently, we were making love and the thing that went through my head was that I was back on the delivery table, giving birth. It was really intense; it was quite terrifying. I had to go through that again to be able to have an or-

gasm. I was afraid that that would happen every time, but it didn't. It's strange, because I didn't experience the giving birth as a sexual experience, but on some level I must have.

Rachel seemed to have to recall the surrender of birth itself to be able to let herself go enough to experience orgasm. To seek pleasure, toward the goal of surrendering one's ego, requires an ego and a sense of oneself as a subject seeking an object. The mother in the first months lacks sufficient sense of her self or of psychic wholeness to do this. Until that wholeness is restored, sexual pleasure seems irrelevant and sexual fulfillment impossible. The mother has been created, in the early months, in the relationship with the infant. But the rest of her self has yet to be restored.

Psychically, I believe, a mother returns to a fairly primitive state, reflecting that of the baby, recalling what Adrienne Rich calls "her own infant connection to her mother." The mother's drives, sexual as well as maternal, are directed toward the infant. Adult sexuality — active and seeking — is incompatible with this state. But as infancy is hardly a permanent condition, so the mother's sexual quiescence has an end. And that end, at five months, is approaching. Faced with pressure from her partner to be herself once more, she may be spurred to discover a little sooner who she has become after all this time.

For many women, though, the extra pressure to get things back to normal simply makes life intolerable. A husband's sexual demands, intruding in this period of confusion, may cause a woman to feel the need to withdraw even further to resist what feels like an assault on her unready ego. She may resist actively by refusing, or with woman's traditional defense of sexual passivity, which leaves her mind almost as undisturbed as her body. Many women in the fifth month feel a desperate desire to be left alone, to escape the desires of the baby and the demands of others, while they begin the task of restoring the adult self. With the adult self, adult sexuality will be resurrected, and the

ego can once again be surrendered. But a woman cannot surrender what she does not yet possess.

The sense of identity that a woman had before she became a
mother has been shaken. Now she begins to try, in the little
time she has available, to recapture her sense of self. Erik Erikson
defines "the sense of ego identity" as "the individual's accrued
confidence that his inner sameness and continuity are matched
by the sameness and continuity of his meaning for others."
Lillian's sudden inability to see herself as the teacher she had
been for fifteen years and Joanne's feeling that she had been
"down a hole for the past five months" attest to the disruption
in their sense of internal continuity. Joanne said:

> ~ I don't remember what I used to do with my time.
> The things I do remember, it seems like a different person
> did them. It's the same thing — I can't believe I ever wore
> those clothes.

The complaints now do not revolve so much on the problems
of management, of how to fit everything in, as they did earlier
and as they may do again. The women were expressing a sense
of loss, and there are two distinct things which have been lost.
One is the symbiotic closeness with the baby; the other is the
woman she was. Both losses contribute to the lack of continuity.
Lillian suffered the loss of an important part of her accustomed
identity; Joanne felt discontinuity with her old self and what
seemed to her the mysterious disappearance of her happy obsession with her daughter. Babies begin to reach out to the
world, and their mothers feel the need to withdraw, to give
themselves a chance to find out what has happened. Several
used the same words: "I just want to be left alone."

As the baby hatches from symbiosis, the mother may find,
returning her attention to herself, that she is confronting a relative stranger. Often her body is not the one she knew, either
during pregnancy or before. Her appearance may be altered not
only because of changes in her body itself but because of changes

in her habits of taking care of herself. A mother in the symbiotic phase has typically little time for attending to her personal needs, and her appearance (and her surroundings, for that matter) may be considerably more disordered than she would usually find tolerable. The disorder is both a symptom and a result of the existence of the symbiotic tie. A woman is simply not as aware of herself as she would ordinarily be. When she begins, then, to look at herself again, she may do so with some dismay. Ellen, who was still carrying an extra 15 pounds of unaccustomed weight, said:

> My body, for the most part, is alien to me. It's an obstruction. I have no time to take care of it. I never even get a chance to go to the bathroom in peace. As little time as I have to collect my thoughts, I have just as little time to experience my body. I feel so chaotic so much of the time with just the details that go into Daniel and the house and work. I've lost the ability to set priorities, a sense of what to do first. It's so overwhelming.

Rachel always functioned best in an orderly environment, but even she found that tendency getting out of hand in the fifth month:

> I get upset now when the least little thing goes wrong or if anything is out of place. I guess I was the same way when I first came home from the hospital, but it seemed to be better for a while. Now I get very resentful of my husband because he's not as compulsive as I am about everything. It's not that I want him to *be* compulsive. It's that I want not to be compulsive and I can't.

The delicate balance of a woman's life at this point is easily disturbed, and the disturbance, however small it may seem to someone else, may be beyond her ability to cope. Her resources of good will and patience — especially for those other than the baby — are shallow and will remain so until she begins to find the resolution of her personal upheaval. It is because these women are psychologically so much on edge that it becomes essential to preserve the structure and the schedule that has been established. Any external breakdown becomes a threat and an intrusion.

The work involved in reestablishing an identity is considerable and cannot be accomplished overnight. Early adolescence, that period of deep confusion and undirected seeking, bears some resemblance to the fifth month of motherhood. That stage of life, for an adolescent, may last for a year or two, sometimes longer. A mother (provided she is past adolescence herself) will get through the recapitulation of this stage in a matter of weeks, but it will be no less painful than it was to be fourteen or fifteen and not know who you were.

Erikson defines two aspects of identity, both necessary for full adulthood. One is the ego identity, the "sense of inner sameness and continuity." The amnesia that typically surrounds the experience of childbirth is the initial disruptive force of the sense of continuity. I discovered, in interviewing mothers, that there was a continuing amnesia, or a misremembering, in the months after the baby was born. Frequently, a woman would refer to something that had taken place earlier — something she or the baby had done or how she had felt in a particular instance. On later checking the interview transcript, I often found that her recollection, a month or two after the event, did not coincide with what she had originally told me. And sometimes she did not remember things at all. Sarah, for example, did not recall her outburst at Jacob when I brought it up three months after the fact. As we discussed the incident, however, it came back to her. She was at least as disturbed by her forgetting as she was by her expression of rage at the baby.

The submergence of the mother in the identification with an infant during symbiosis is in every possible sense normal, provided that it ends. But a glance at the abnormal may help to illuminate what happens to a woman during and after symbiosis. Identity diffusion, a pathological condition which affects some psychotics and neurotics, to some extent describes a new mother. David DeLevita lists seven characteristics of identity diffusion in the schizophrenic:

1. onset between the ages of 16 and 24
2. disturbance in engagement to others, isolation
3. disturbance in sexual identity
4. disturbance in time perspective
5. inability to concentrate and to derive satisfaction from activity
6. characteristic family structure
7. symbiotic sibling relationship

Curiously, four of these seven — 2, 3, 4, and 5 — describe the mother in symbiosis.

There is another relationship which has been described as symbiotic: that between the schizophrenic patient and the therapist. The schizophrenic, unable to differentiate reality from unreality, tries to merge with the therapist and seems sometimes to draw strength, or some measure of sanity, from the therapist. H. Searles, a psychoanalyst who has had long experience in treating schizophrenics, has written:

> . . . both patient and therapist have unconscious resistance to their emergence from the symbiotic phase of their work: for each of them to emerge from this symbiosis means not the resumption of his familiar sense of individual identity, but the experiencing, rather, of a new individual identity — an identity which has been changed by the symbiotic relationship with the other person.

With a change of words "patient and therapist" to "infant and mother," this is a fair description of what faces a mother (and a baby, for that matter) as the sixth month approaches.

The second aspect of identity that Erikson defines, the "self-identity . . . emerges from experiences in which temporarily confused selves are successfully reintegrated in an ensemble of roles which also secure social recognition." A woman is a mother, but not the contented mother that she was or thinks she should be; she is a wife, but not deeply interested in her husband, rather removed from him, in fact, as he has probably begun to point out; a working woman, but her attention to her work is not what it was, or she finds that she is bored or not doing a good job, or begins to suspect that she is in the wrong field; a sexual being, but her interest in sex is difficult even to recall.

Reintegrating these roles — regaining the sense of self and integrating it with the fact of motherhood — is the central task of the second half of the first nine months. In that time the woman's role in her family will stabilize, as will her understanding of that role; her status at work or in her community will crystallize into that of woman-who-is-also-a-mother; her own sense of herself will emerge to incorporate all that she was with the mother that she has become.

CHAPTER 5

THE SIXTH AND SEVENTH MONTHS
Coming Back to Me

1

"IT'S BEEN," said Ellen, when Daniel was six months old, "a moratorium from life." Ellen by this time had been back at work part-time for four months. Nonetheless, she felt that something had ended and something new had begun.

By the sixth month of the baby's life most mothers have lost interest in the minutiae of baby care and feeding. When I asked mothers to describe their daily routines, the mothers in symbiosis invariably told me about the baby's day in inordinate detail. They complained of having no time to read, to take a shower, sometimes even to go to the bathroom. The baby, helpless as she was, completely absorbed her mother's time and energies. By the sixth month the answers to the same question were often like this one from Ellen:

> ∿ I'm still nursing, so I feed him upstairs first and then bring him down to the kitchen for his breakfast. He has a nap around ten or ten-thirty and sleeps for an hour or so, eats lunch at twelve, has a nap around two or three, supper at six, goes to bed about eight, and sleeps through the night.

Taking care of the baby has become much more automatic: "I can do it with my eyes closed," commented one mother, who three months earlier had been unable to stop gazing at the baby. In the sixth month there is a remarkable increase in the baby's

121

physical activity. Often, in this stage, the mothers would try to schedule interviews for times when the baby would be napping or in someone else's care. While the babies in the sixth month couldn't yet crawl, many could creep and almost all could roll over. Thus most of them, with some difficulty, could get from place to place and needed more watching than was necessary a month earlier. They could sit fairly comfortably, some needing support and some not. Sitting in a high chair, a baby would drop a toy, watch it fall, then beg for it to be retrieved.

Holding a baby of this age in your lap does not diminish her level of activity. She tries to stand or to climb down and then back up. She pokes at your eyes, mouths your nose, grabs your earring, and makes it impossible to see or hear another adult, since all this poking and prying is accompanied by babbling and crowing without letup.

A baby may prefer to sit by herself near mother's feet, rather than on her lap. The bottle is still usually given to the baby in arms, though some are learning to hold the bottle and a few already insist on doing so for themselves, at least some of the time. Most babies, by the age of six months, are fed solids while sitting in a high chair. They still want to be held when they are tired or distressed, and there are many moments of relaxed cuddling. But infants in arms are more often active and so interested in the world around them that they often prefer to be held so that they are facing out and not toward mother.

By seven months, the baby will slide off her mother's lap altogether and wriggle or crawl across the room, often approaching mischief, picking up little things from the floor and invariably putting them into her mouth. She may return briefly to her mother's feet, and may try to pull herself into her lap, but no sooner is she there than she slides off to another adventure.

Accompanying the new independence is a waning of interest in the breast, which often coincides with the first appearance of teeth. Many babies seem to prefer the more autonomous style of drinking from a bottle they can hold themselves, or even from a cup, inefficient as most of them are at that. Many mothers, recognizing the lack of interest in the breast, take this opportunity to begin to wean the baby.

Pediatrician T. Berry Brazelton, in *Infants and Mothers: Differences in Development*, has identified three points in the first year when the infant's interest in breastfeeding begins to diminish. The first coincides with the baby's widening interest in the world in the fifth month. "The second," Brazelton writes, "accompanies the tremendous motor spurt of seven months. The third occurs between nine and twelve months." Since the major nutritional and health benefits of breastfeeding seem to diminish after the first few months of life, there seems little reason, unless there is a strong family history of allergy or unless a mother finds breastfeeding considerably more convenient than bottle-feeding, not to take advantage of the baby's waning interest at these points. I noticed, in fact, that many mothers, without specific advice, dropped one or two regular nursing sessions in the fifth month, another around the seventh, and allowed the baby to wean herself entirely shortly after nine months. This gradual process seems to be a good deal less stressful for everyone concerned than a sudden and complete weaning.

The babies no longer seem so fragile. Their ability to control their heads and trunks, as well as their hands and arms, make them seem capable of surviving. Their signals are also clearer. A hungry baby can gesture toward the bottle; the tired one rubs her eyes or pulls her ear. The mother has more confidence that someone else may be nearly as capable as she to interpret those signals and is often more willing to have others participate in the baby's care. She is more confident that she will be able to tell, on returning, if the baby has been happy and well treated during her absence.

Alice's daughter Maya had been cared for by Alice's aunt (who cared for several other children as well) from the time the baby was three months old, when Alice went back to school. At six months Alice realized that the baby was reacting badly to the atmosphere in her aunt's home:

~ She was always crying and cranky, and the minute she got home, at five or six, she'd sleep. I had to wake her up at nine at night, just to say "Hello." Now, she has completely, *completely* changed. She's just so calm. She doesn't cry like that any more, she plays by herself, her whole personality has changed. I think it was too crazy at my aunt's; there were too many kids in too small a space, and I think she was nervous. I was going through all kinds of changes, and people were saying it's not your aunt, it's probably something else, and you're just putting it on that, but intuitively, I knew.

Along with the baby's improved ability to communicate, in the sixth and seventh months her sense of herself as a separate person and her awareness of others continues to expand. She begins to become fascinated by the distinction between what is part of a person and what is not — hence the interest in what can be removed (eyeglasses) and what cannot (hair). She is also fascinated with her reflection in the mirror, although experiments show that she does not know that it is a reflection of herself and will not know that for another six months or more. A baby at six or seven months will put her fingers in her own mouth, then into the mouth of the person facing her. The sensation of her mouth when her fingers are in it is of course different from that when her fingers are in someone else's mouth, and the recognition of differences like these helps her to distinguish herself from others. The mimicking that babies do, which at first was only of expressions and gestures, becomes more active and complex. Ellen described a scene typical of babies at this age:

~ Whenever I give him food now, he tries to feed me, besides trying to feed himself. If I pick up a piece of something in my fingers and put it in his mouth, the next thing he'll do is to pick up something and try to put it in mine.

There is general agreement, among those who have studied the question of identity and the sense of self, that a human being must be able to recognize others before she can construct a sense of her self. Erik Erikson, who has written a great deal about identity (though little about its earliest beginnings), has written recently that "there can be no 'I' without an 'Other,' no 'we' without a shared 'Other.' That, in fact, is the first revelation of the life cycle, when the maternal person's eyes shiningly recognize us even as we begin to recognize her."

The game of peek-a-boo, which usually starts with an adult (or child) covering her own face — a gesture the six-month-old will rapidly learn to mimic — and which can keep a baby amused apparently for hours, is more than just a game. For the baby it means that "the baby has a memory of someone he loves, and her or his image is fixed enough in his mind and secure enough in his feelings for him to try a short separation under his control. It also means that he has a sense of his mother's permanence . . . and even anticipates the joy of recalling her."

In order to begin to prefer one or several people above all others (which is necessary in order to be considered emotionally normal in our society) it is necessary to be with a diverse group of others and to learn to distinguish among them. While that may appear to be self-evident, it has not been so apparent to everyone. John Bowlby, in all his writing about attachment formation, stresses the importance of the mother and the continuous relationship with her. In his view, only the mother is necessary. Bowlby's mother and infant have no social context of any significance, and their relationship seems to develop in an almost perfect vacuum. Even fathers run far, far behind:

> . . . the child's relation to his mother . . . is without doubt in ordinary circumstances by far his most important relationship during these years. In the young child's eyes father plays second fiddle and his value increases only as the child's vulnerability to deprivation increases. Nevertheless, as the

illegitimate child knows, fathers have their uses even in
infancy. Not only do they provide for their wives to enable
them to devote themselves unrestrictedly to the care of the
infant and toddler, but, by providing love and companionship, they support her emotionally and help her maintain
that harmonious and contented mood in the aura of which
the infant thrives. . . . [T]herefore, while continual reference will be made to the mother-child relation, little will be
said of the father-child relation; his value as the economic
and emotional support of the mother will be assumed.

Bowlby's message is that the primary tie to the mother, which
he believes is formed in the second half-year of life (although
recent evidence, as we have seen, indicates that this tie is formed
much earlier), is necessarily the strongest tie that the child will
form, at least until the Oedipal crisis several years later. It is
also posited as the *only* necessary tie for the child's adequate
emotional development. Bowlby, and the attachment theorists
who have followed him, rely heavily on monkey studies to prove
their case.

Monkeys reared without others of their kind do not develop
normally. They do not exhibit normal social behavior nor, later
in life, do they show normal mating behavior. Since in the wild
the social group is necessary for protection, and since mating is
obviously necessary for the continuation of the species, the monkey reared in isolation is not functional in an evolutionary sense.
While the original studies of monkeys reared in complete isolation from others attributed their social maladjustment to the
fact that they had been reared without their mothers, the need
for more than one "Other" has now been confirmed, at least for
monkeys. While it is tricky, at best, to extrapolate from monkeys
to humans, it is much easier to manipulate the environment of
a monkey than that of a human being, so the monkey studies
provide the only available evidence about certain conditions.

Harry Harlow, whose work is quoted by everyone interested
in attachment formation, in his recent work (with Stephen J.

Suomi) has pointed out that a monkey's developmental needs are more complex than was earlier realized. They found that to produce a severely maladjusted monkey, they didn't have to isolate it from *all* other monkeys. "We have found that monkeys reared with biological mothers but denied the opportunity to interact with peers early in life also fail to develop appropriate patterns of interactive behavior when finally exposed to peers." While these mother-reared monkeys do not sit, rocking and clasping themselves and sucking on their hands and feet, as do the monkeys raised completely alone, Harlow and Suomi describe them as "contact-shy." They don't play with other monkeys and "are likely to be hyperaggressive." And when they grow up they often do not mate.

While Harlow's earlier studies — the ones that showed that monkeys reared without their mothers did not become well-adjusted adult monkeys — have been cited again and again by Bowlby and more popular writers on childrearing to prove that mothers are essential for babies' normal development, this later work is rarely mentioned. There is, however, a still small but growing number of child development experts who are willing to argue that contact with peers is as necessary for human babies as it is for rhesus monkeys. Michael Lewis and Leonard Rosenblum, the former working with infants and children and the latter with several varieties of monkeys, write in the introduction to a collection titled *Friendship and Peer Relations:*

> The idea that the mother-infant dyad, for example, is sufficient in and of itself for the young child and that opportunity for active peer interactions may be substantially delayed and then only intermittently afforded . . . may have important sequelae in terms of the subsequent functioning of the individual and of the society.

Mothers have been persuaded, in the past forty years or so, that they are not only necessary but sufficient for their babies' development. The corollary to this belief, in terms of peer relations, has been that babies and young children have no interest in one another and do not and need not play together until the age of three years, when nursery school is advised for the child of a conscientious mother.

By the sixth or seventh month any mother of more than one child knows different. Alice, who was a graduate student in psychology, commented when her daughter Maya was six-and-a-half months old:

> ~ They *always* talk about attachment in terms of the mother. I'm not trying to put myself down, but nobody has talked about attachment to fathers, attachment to siblings. The fact is that nobody in this whole country raises their kids just mother and child. There are millions of working women, the rich have nannies, working women have day-care centers and grandmas. The model of development, though, is still based on that mother-child dyad, while I'm sure the majority of kids are not raised that way. All you have to do is have one other kid — another child.

Earlier in the infant's life, when asked about the relationship of an older child and a new baby, the mother invariably reported on the older child's reaction to the infant. By the sixth month, however, whatever the earlier situation, the mothers responded by telling me about the baby's response to her older brother or sister. When Maya was six-and-a-half months old, Alice told me that her two children had just begun sharing a room. Referring to her son, who was nearly four, she said, "Kareem just does whatever he usually does, and Maya sits and watches him and laughs and laughs hysterically."

Babies by this age will initiate play with older children and can play simple games with them. The babies love peek-a-boo and I-drop-it-you-pick-it-up, and a willing sibling can amuse them with these and similar reciprocal games almost indefinitely. Many babies are obviously extremely fond of their siblings, and there are reports in the literature of babies who show strong and early preferences for a particular brother or sister, even over the mother or father.

At one interview I watched the baby sitting in her infant seat as her older sister arrived home from nursery school. The baby showed the greatest animation I had seen from her in the two hours I'd been there. She crowed, laughed, smiled, waved her arms and legs, and seemed generally overcome with joy when her sister approached and hugged and kissed her. The sister lifted her from the infant seat, and they sat companionably on the floor while the older sister named the pictures in a book for the younger.

Babies react with particular delight even to strange babies and children, when adult strangers evoke simply an attentive or even a fearful response. The reasons for babies' recognition of other babies as being like themselves and not threatening are not really known, although a number of clever experiments have been devised to try to discover the answers. It has been reasoned that a child's small size, being close to the size of the baby, might cue the baby that the child is unlikely to do her harm. It has also been argued that the difference in the usual proportions of an adult's face and a child's face (for instance, the child's larger eyes and higher forehead) might be the cue that allowed the baby to distinguish between them.

A series of experiments was conducted at the Educational Testing Service in Princeton, New Jersey, wherein babies were approached by unfamiliar adults of both sexes and then by children of both sexes. The findings are preliminary, but they do confirm that the babies react more positively to children than to adults, and more positively to females than to males. The reason here may be that babies are simply more accustomed to women than they are to men and are therefore less likely to be afraid of them.

To try to determine whether the babies were responding only to size, rather than to facial cues, the experimenters had a small adult, a woman about the size of the children used in the experiment, approach the babies. They found that, while the infants did not show fear of the small adult, they "smiled and reached toward the children but not toward the small adult. The most characteristic response to the latter was prolonged and concentrated staring with little movement or affect exhibited. This seems to indicate that the size-face discrepancy present in the small adult is perceived by the infant although it does not produce distress."

To what extent, if any, the baby at this age (the youngest subjects in these experiments were seven months old) has a sense or a picture of the self that allows her to evaluate other children as being "like me," we do not know. But if human beings are like other animals, so that "like me" is a positive valuation, then these babies may already have some sense that there is a likeness to themselves in the other children and an unlikeness in the adults. If the first stage in the formation of identity was the mirror of the mother's face, and if in that mirror the baby learned what she is like, she has now somehow begun to learn what she is unlike. She has compounded her sense of identity to the point that she can distinguish that, while she is a human being like other human beings, she is more like some than others.

The baby in some way sees herself as more like other children than she is like adults, presumably including her mother. By the beginning of her second half-year she has begun to realize that she is not only separate from her mother, but different from her, too. The mothers realize the same thing, of course. The mere fact that a baby prefers to sit alone, instead of in her mother's lap, forces a mother into the recognition that something rather fundamental has changed. She must now begin to acknowledge that she and the baby are separate and different from each other. The mother's drive to reestablish her own sense of who she is now begins to take on strength.

The mothers I interviewed in the sixth month expressed the same sense of discontinuity — the feeling of "Where have I been all this time?" — that they did in the fifth month, but now it begins to acquire content and direction, and a feeling now takes hold that she must *do* something. One symptom of the mother's attempt to reestablish continuity for herself is the determination at last to restore her body to its prepregnant size and shape. One woman, who had wallowed in symbiosis after a particularly anxious pregnancy, by six months was newly concerned with herself:

✍ I was always very thin, so it's hard for me to accept myself this way. My body is so out of shape it's just horrible. I never was big on exercise, but now I've got to take off 15 pounds, and exercise is the only way I'm ever going to firm up.

Her tone was one of disgust and impatience with herself. Even those who were not overweight, however, had something to say about their bodies. Rosemary, who was small and slight and looked quite trim, said, "It's not so much the weight, because I've weighed this before, but I never *looked* like this before. I had a very tiny waist and never an ounce of fat on my mid-section."

The need to get back to the way she used to look is symptomatic of other changes which are less obvious but nonetheless real and compelling. Shirley, who complained that she was going to have to begin to exercise, had had several miscarriages before finally carrying her daughter to term. She was thrilled and relieved to be a mother and to have a bright and healthy infant to take care of. Symbiosis passed with scarcely a ripple in the surface of their well-matched relationship. When I saw Shirley when her daughter Patty was just six months old, she was still delighted with the baby, but wanted to talk about herself. She, like the others, felt the need to take some action:

✍ I'm freer of her and she's freer of me, so I have to do something. I'm going to take a sewing class next month, but even right now I have to find something to do and some other girls to be with during the day. Now what I'm trying to do is just arrange babysitting. . . . I like taking care of her, but there's something missing. I feel dull, and I've got to find what to do without going back to work.

Many women by this time have gone back to jobs that they do not especially like, out of economic necessity or because their maternity leave (if they had any) is up and they cannot afford to lose the job they had. Many, like Shirley, are not interested in going back to the jobs they had, which are frequently routine, unrewarding, and poorly paid, if they can possibly afford not to. Shirley and her husband lived upstairs in his parents' two-family house. The rent was low. Shirley had saved most of her salary for several years before the baby came, just so that she would not have to return to work immediately. Shirley's identity was not tied up with the job she had held, and the only thing about working outside the home that attracted her was the social life it provided. But having no job to reinforce her sense of identity as an autonomous adult, she was faced with creating new activities.

The women who still insisted that the baby was enough, that they wanted nothing more, were, by six months, exceptions. (They are discussed in the next chapter.) For the most part, the mothers were looking for something for themselves, or, if they already had something, were seeking something more or something different. Nonetheless, there is an almost universal ambivalence about leaving the baby and returning to the world. Carol, a mother of two, a professional with a high-powered and demanding career, was well aware of her mixed feelings:

> ~ I already miss the intimacy of those very first weeks. You just don't feel it with anybody else. On one hand, I know that I couldn't be home all the time, but someplace there is a residual something that says you are not spending enough time with your children; you *miss* your children. It's not that the kids are being deprived — I don't mean to say that — but there's something *I* am not getting.

Rosemary, the much younger mother of a first son, after working for her first full week said:

∾ I have had days when I just wanted to be away from him, but if this week was a test, it was a lot for me. I really felt like he'd forgotten who I am. That's bullshit of course. I project a lot of my need into him. I thought of him already going to camp, and how much I would miss him.

Rosemary, who does free-lance art work, was in the enviable position of being able to establish her own work schedule. After the experience of spending a full week at work, she made the reasonable decision to spend no more than three days a week working in the future, in order to be able to spend about half her days with the baby. Still, like the other women coming out of symbiosis, she was not satisfied with what she had. She was making plans to return to school part-time in a few months, to have, as she said, "something for myself."

The new mother now also begins to hear and to respond to the demands made by other members of her family, in a way she could not before. Her role as mother to her other children is resumed. Older children, especially if they are only two or three years older than the new baby, often have a very hard time in the early months. Anne, with an infant daughter and a three-year-old son, had great difficulty living up to the very high standards she set for herself and had to contend with a very angry little boy:

∾ He never tries to hurt the baby; he lets it all out on me. He's constantly trying to provoke me into a fight. He asks for something he knows he can't have, and then has a fit when I tell him he can't have it. It's very hard to control myself. And whenever I'm nursing, he climbs all over me.

Sometimes the older child's hostility toward the baby is hidden from the mother. One woman rejoiced over the wonderful relationship her two-and-a-half-year-old had with his baby brother:

~ There's just no sign of any jealousy. He just *loves* the baby. He sits on my lap while I'm feeding the baby, and sometimes he wants a bottle, too, but he's just always sweet with his brother.

When this mother went into the house for a moment, leaving me and the two children on the porch, the older boy, thinking that I was not watching, seized the opportunity to deliver a vicious kick to his baby brother's shin. The baby cried, and his brother, eyeing me, began to comfort him. When his mother returned, she smiled approvingly at the affectionate scene.

By the sixth month, most of the mothers were taking advantage of the baby's ability to amuse herself, and of their own decreased absorption in the baby, to begin to spend more time with their older children. Carol, whose older son Joshua was three, and whose job made apparently endless demands on her time, said:

~ I suddenly realized that, on some level, I've been neglecting Josh. I am making a tremendous effort to be home to put him to bed as many nights of the week as possible, and I try to do things with him that are special to us. He tells me stories and I draw pictures to illustrate them.

Alice was having a similar experience with her older son:

~ I had the feeling he had been tugging at my sleeve for a long time, and I had been trying to ignore it. Now, after she goes to bed in the evening is my time with him. I don't know why I didn't think of it sooner.

2

How a woman feels about her husband depends heavily on his attitude and behavior toward the baby. In this society, until quite recently, men were not really expected to have much to do with their children until those children were well past infancy. John

Bowlby's assumption that a father's job was to furnish emotional and financial support for his wife so that she would be free to mother was widely held, and it was far from uncommon to hear a man say, without guilt or shame, that he had no interest in his children before they were old enough to talk.

A 1971 study "wired" the fathers of three-month-old infants to determine accurately the amount of time that the fathers spent interacting with their infants. The average father in the study spent 37.7 seconds a day doing what was being measured. The highest individual figure was 10 minutes, 26 seconds. I cite this with mixed feelings, because while it certainly does reflect a pervasive social phenomenon, it does a disservice to the men who have participated in the revolution of the past decade and a half. The most casual glance at any middle-class community in the 1980s reveals that many fathers spend a great deal more time with their babies and children than used to be the case. In my own study there was a vast range of behavior shown by the fathers.

Joanne's husband was an electrician. He put in long, hard hours and earned enough that Joanne could stay home with the baby:

> He comes home, and he's tired, and he doesn't really want to talk, and I don't have anything to talk about but the baby, and he's interested for about five minutes and then he doesn't want to hear it. Then I get resentful about everything he asks for, and I think, "I'm tired, too. Why doesn't he get it himself?"

Even in a very traditional marriage like this one, however, some expectations have changed:

> I told Joe that I want him to spend time every night with the baby, because I don't want her growing up with the father that I grew up with. My father was just a total blank to all of us. If we went to him with anything, he'd say, "Go ask your mother." So Joe spends time, he helps,

but not to the point where it's a relief for me. He still doesn't know what she eats or when or where anything is. He's always asking where's the diapers, or how much milk goes in the bottle. So then I get up, and after I get everything out, he'll sit there and feed her, and as soon as she gets cranky, he says I don't know what to do with her. Last Sunday, he said he would take care of her while I went and saw my girlfriend who just had a baby. So he took her to his mother's, and his mother and his sister took care of her. When I got there, he gave her to me to feed and he went off with his brother.

The baby's effect on Joanne's relationship with her husband had been far from positive. Before the baby, she said,

~ We were never home, even if we just went for a ride. We'd eat out when we wanted to. We had money; we were both working. Now, if he wants to go out to eat on Sunday morning, if we take her, I end up holding her, and I don't enjoy myself, so I stay home. He's resentful because we don't get out much. Before, we always did things together, but now, even when we're away from the baby, she's right there between us.

Even in traditional relationships, the father's disengagement wasn't always so disastrous. Shirley's husband, working an evening shift, saw his baby even less than Joanne's husband did. By the time he came home, the baby was in bed, but Shirley didn't expect much of him, as far as fathering was concerned, and didn't seem to mind:

~ It's nice that the baby's asleep when Frank comes home. That way, we get to have some time alone together. I wait dinner until he gets here, and it's always nice and quiet. Sometimes he plays with her in the morning after he gets up.

I asked whether Frank was jealous or resentful of her attention to the baby.

No. He thinks I'm a good mother, and he likes her, and he likes the way I take care of her. He's really glad that he makes enough so I can stay home. That was very important to him, even though I saved a lot so we could manage without me working.

Frank was rather unusual in being an almost perfect example of Bowlby's ideal father, happy to be able to support his family and largely uninvolved with his daughter. A conflict between traditional arrangements and modern expectations was more usual. One father made this comment:

It must've been pretty nice in the old days when all you had to do was provide a good living. Now you have to do that and child care besides. When I go to work, Lucy seems to feel like I'm abandoning the house. I'm expected to spend twenty-four hours a day doing child care. My work doesn't count.

(No woman I interviewed and no mother I have spoken to under any circumstances has *ever* referred to taking care of her children as "doing child care" or "babysitting." Many of the fathers, however, did.) This father did quite a lot of child care and had what appeared to be a warm and nurturant relationship with both his infant and five-year-old sons. He continued: "The situation is very tense because we all have to improvise in so many different ways."

Many mothers and fathers express similar feelings. The stress in these families arises not because of some ill will on the part of the father or excessive demand on the part of the mother. The fact is that caring for an infant is exhausting work, physically and emotionally draining, and often boring besides. A man coming home at the end of a long work day may be understandably reluctant to spend the next two or three hours caring for an infant who may well be particularly cranky at that time of day. The baby's mother, on the other hand, having spent the last eight or nine or ten hours with the baby, is, equally understandably, frantic for relief. As one mother said, "Two people are just not enough to care for one baby. Everything I don't do, he has to do; and everything he doesn't do, I have to."

Our expectations in this realm have far outstripped our society's willingness or ability to meet them. Adequate maternity and paternity leaves, part-time work that doesn't leave the worker in poverty, job sharing (to say nothing of nannies, nursery maids, housekeepers, and quality day care for infants) all might alleviate the problem. As it is, even couples who are committed to doing things fifty-fifty quickly discover that his one well-paid, full-time job can support a family of three or four better than her one not-so-well-paid full-time job, or any part-time job that either of them might be able to get. The problem of integrating marriage and babies is a social one, but no social solution seems imminent.

Some couples did find individual solutions. Dick had a business which he ran from their home, and he shared many of the everyday baby-care responsibilities with his wife Elaine. They both stressed the positive aspects of his involvement with their son. Dick said:

> ~ I think what happens — what I see in Kenny anyway — is that he knows that more than one person can satisfy some of his primary needs, whereas if your child only has the experience of his mother, then that's a very exclusive relationship, and I would think it would be very hard on the kid if someone else came along to take care of him. It would have to be very scary. Kenny's expectation is that whoever comes in to take care of him when he's in distress will help him.

Elaine said:

> ~ I think that in many ways having the baby has brought us closer together. You learn about another side of the person. Dick has more respect for me, seeing what I went through with childbirth, and I know I have more respect

for him, seeing how he's adjusted to being a father. Both of those were things that we were very, very frightened of.

The question of whether fathers can mother or how good they are as mother-substitutes is one that has been raised only very recently in our society. Since lower animals have been repeatedly used to demonstrate various things about mothering behavior (especially to prove that mothers are necessary), we can begin by looking at what the lower animals have to show us about whether fathers can exhibit mothering behavior. Rats, as we have seen, if exposed to baby rats, begin to mother them. No one, of course, is surprised when a rat gives birth and then does all the appropriate things with her young. It's all quite "natural," and has been attributed to her producing the right hormones. But if you expose virgin females to newborn rats for a few hours a day over a couple of weeks, they too start to act like mothers. They can't suckle the young, but they crouch over them, lick them, retrieve them and build nests, just like regular mother rats.

The team that first did these experiments hypothesized that just being near the baby rats might stimulate hormone production in the virgin females, and that the presence of hormones would cause them to behave as they did. They repeated their experiments with virgin females whose ovaries had been removed, so that the main source of female hormone was eliminated. The rats acted just like the original ones. Then they removed the rats' pituitary glands, and the results were again the same. They tried it with males, then with castrated males, and they kept getting the same results: When an adult rat was placed in contact with newborn rats, nearly all the adults displayed "maternal" behavior.

As for the monkeys, while it is true that *rhesus* monkeys cling to their mothers and prefer their mothers over any other female, and that an infant removed from its mother will protest and become depressed and withdrawn, the same is not true for all species of monkeys. Among bonnet monkeys, for instance, infants are handed around among a group of females. If the mother is removed, after a short time the infant will attach itself to another female. When the mother returns, the infant will return to her, but without the excessive clinging and displays of anger that a reunited rhesus infant shows. And among gibbons, who form monogamous pairs, the male and female spend about equal amounts of time carrying their young. So it appears that we can draw any conclusion we want, or perhaps no conclusion at all, from the lower animals.

While many human fathers participate much more than ever before in the lives of their infants, there are still very, very few who spend as much time with them as does the average mother. Certainly, we know that fathers are perfectly capable of *doing* everything that mothers do, with the exception of breastfeeding, though they may do them a little differently. Brazelton and other investigators have found differences in approach between mothers and fathers with their infants. The fathers tend to keep a little greater distance, to touch the infants less, to poke and tickle instead of stroking and patting as a mother does. It seems, though, that the fathers in these experiments were not ones who spent as much time with the babies as the mothers did.

I thought that there might be something to be learned from fathers who were with their babies half-time or more. I wanted to know whether those fathers became at all like the mothers, not in terms of their *behavior*, but in terms of their feelings. Did they, for instance, enter a symbiotic relationship with the baby and then have to struggle out from it? Were they as engrossed with the infant, or did they retain some of the traditional father's distance? What role models did they have? What impact did a father's involvement with his infant have on his relationship with the baby's mother? Did the mother and father fight for control — did they worry about which of them the infant loved best? I interviewed only five men who met my criterion, so the answers that I found are tentative. Nonetheless, they seem suggestive and certainly offer an area for investigation.

Fathers who are present when their children are born become engrossed in watching the newborn. One researcher found that new fathers behaved much the way new mothers did in the first hour after birth: They looked at the baby, stroked it, talked softly to it. The fathers I interviewed who were present when their children were born described themselves as "amazed," "overwhelmed," "euphoric."

The first month or two, for the full-time father, seems nearly as draining as it is for the full-time mother. Most, in that period, (like many of the fathers who were back at work) had the glazed expression and drooping eyelids typical of anyone suffering extreme sleep deprivation. But the stay-at-home fathers seemed to be experiencing the kind of anxiety that is usually unique to new mothers.

Alex, who was at the end of a fellowship, decided that the money would stretch for a few months when his first child was born. Alex worried whether his son was getting enough to eat, worried about whether his wife's anxiety might be interfering with her milk supply, worried about the baby getting hit by objects falling from buildings. All this anxiety soon translated itself into a pervasive sense of responsibility. When the baby was about three months old, he began waking regularly at six A.M. At first, since the baby didn't seem to need to be fed at that hour, Alex would get up and play with him, since the baby was "very vocal early in the morning." After a few weeks, though, Alex found getting up so early difficult and unpleasant:

> ∽ Now, I wake up just a little and see that he's wide awake and staring around, and I think, "If only I could wake up enough to talk to him." I've been brooding about this. It's complete craziness, I'm sure, but I feel that he's getting bored and blasé, and less interested in talking. It seemed like he was developing rapidly, and then he leveled out.

At three-and-a-half months, the height of the symbiotic period for most mothers, Alex said:

~ I know I don't like to be absent. I spent a lot of time fixing up his room, and after five or six hours of painting, I thought, "Geez, it's five or six hours I haven't been near him, six hours I'll never get back again." When I'm away, I have a lot of stray thoughts and a lot of them are about Andy. When I'm not with him, I think about him.

Doug, who is a free-lance writer, was able to arrange to be at home, and his wife Alicia returned to her job part-time when their daughter was just a few weeks old. When the baby was nearly five months old, Doug told me:

~ I find that I can't get any work done at all. That was a surprise for me, because I thought that she'd sleep and I'd get all this work done. I figured, it won't make any difference. Alicia will be at work, and I'll be at work, and it'll be fine. I don't know if she knows I don't want her to go to sleep or what, but she never wants to sleep during the day when I have her. If I get her to sleep, she'll wake up in an hour, and I can't get my concentration up in an hour. I can't write anything.

I asked what he did all day.

~ I spend most of my time playing with her, because whenever she does anything, I can't stand the thought of wasting her time, her lying around in the crib being lonely, so I stop what I'm doing and play with her. It's more compelling than a gorgeous woman lying on a bed and waving to you to come to the bed. Then you could say, this can wait, maybe, but not a baby that's smiling at you, or crying. Once she's into doing something, it's even more disruptive to my day than when she's upset. When she's upset, my inclination is to try to get her to go to sleep, so I'll feed her or diaper her and than I'll sing to her and carry her around for a while, and hopefully she'll go off, and that's my aim.

But when she's up playing, my aim is to keep her going, and she'll go for hours.

Alicia, too, had work that she was supposed to do at home. Doug said:

↶ I wouldn't have been able to understand her dilemma, if I hadn't been taking care of the baby. I might've thought, "Oh, she just can't get anything done because she can't get herself focused." But now I can see it, because I can't either.

This couple, both home part-time and away part-time, seemed remarkably uncompetitive. Alex and his wife, Ruth, both at home all the time with the baby, started to get on each other's nerves.

↶ We carp at each other a lot over really tiny things. I don't know that it's so much a desire to do the best thing for him, or if it's really competition. I think it's probably some of both. We have different philosophies, Ruth and I. Her idea is that we should both be totally consistent in the way we handle him. I'm much more flexible than she is, much less regimented. Deep down, I feel that I handle things very naturally, more so than Ruth does, so I feel that whatever way I do things is well thought out and reasonable, but Ruth frequently objects to things I do.

This sort of competitiveness was not likely to be a problem when only one parent was in charge of the baby. I asked Alex why he had decided to stay home while the baby was small.

↶ I thought being around Andrew I could make sure he would be raised the way I wanted him to. I have very definite ideas about children. Now I'm beginning to feel I'd like to be a little less involved, partly because my anxiety about Ruth's mothering — well, she's a good mother. I didn't know that she would be. I guess I always thought that I would be a better mother than Ruth.

Doug stayed home because it was reasonably convenient for him to do so, because he wanted the experience of being close to his baby daughter, and because he and Alicia had made a serious commitment to try to divide their responsibilities evenly. He felt lucky that things had worked out well:

> ❧ If I had any other kind of job, I would've missed this unforgettable part of my child's life. That's what happens to most men; they have absolutely no alternative. I think they're really jealous and I think they have to deny it and make jokes about it. I felt really jealous of the relationship that Alicia had with Miranda through nursing. I felt really great when I could give her a bottle, because then she'd look at me the same way.

The parents who had found a way to share the care and responsibility for the child, even those like Alex and Ruth who were often at odds, did not feel as estranged from each other as did the other couples at six months. In fact, their experience seemed to be quite the opposite. When I asked about the state of Doug's relationship with Alicia, he told me:

> ❧ It's hard to know how much the relationship has actually changed, because right now it's so minute-to-minute, but I feel like we've gotten a lot closer. We're very lucky that we can relate through Miranda. We're both real tired, but she helps us jump the gap.

All the men who stayed home felt that they were privileged to be able to do so. Whether their children will bear out the theories of Nancy Chodorow and Dorothy Dinnerstein, that children who are reared *in infancy* by both women and men will be profoundly different in their attitudes toward women and men and the world in general, remains to be seen. These children are, after all, true pioneers, as are their fathers. They follow no models. It must be pointed out, however, that they were, to a man, happy with the choice they had made. It must also be noted, less happily, that two of the five full-time fathers I interviewed, when they had second children, had full-time work that did not permit extended time off, and they both slipped,

with some ease and some regret, back into a much more traditional pattern of fathering.

3

By the sixth month, many of the women found themselves able
to make changes that had seemed impossible only a few weeks
earlier. Elaine had been on leave from her job as a psychiatric
nurse since a couple of weeks before her son Kenneth was born.
The week before he was seven months old, she handed in her
resignation. When I first saw her, she told me that she had not
been happy in the job and was reluctant to go back, since it
entailed considerable commuting and would keep her away from
home more than forty hours a week, but she had not given it
up until now.

   ✧ I finally handed in my resignation. It was a whole
wrench. It was kind of like my security blanket, and I said,
well, at least if something doesn't come up, I can always
go back there. I finally realized I was using that as an excuse
for not doing anything. A lot of my energies were still emotionally there and weren't getting invested in any other
situation.

It was not until this point that Elaine felt sure enough of herself to be able to make this change. For most of the mothers
change seemed, for the first time since the baby was born, not
only possible but welcome. The women who had no intention
or need to return to jobs were looking for recreational or social
activities; the ones who wanted work began to look for it, and
the ones who had jobs or careers, no matter how satisfying,
began to look for something in addition, something they could
call their own.

Ellen, who had been working for four months, saw that the
"moratorium from life" was ended.

~~ I'm struggling with being ready for going out into the world again. I find I'm reading the paper. It's really been a long time that I haven't been interested in anything out there. I've gone to work and come home, but there hasn't been a lot of time for me, and I haven't really resented it until now. I'm beginning to work on ways to find something else. I'm not sure what it is, but I'm feeling the need for something.

Rosemary, who lived in a traditional family, in a conservative community, had decided to try to finish college, though she had not yet figured out how she was going to juggle home, husband, baby, school, work, child care, and the need for additional income. I asked what part of her life she found most satisfying, and a gesture encompassed her home, her husband's favorite chair, her baby.

~~ I feel this part of my life is most satisfying now, but I already feel like I need some other satisfaction. I feel I'm getting dumber — that's the best way I can describe it. I feel I need more direction to go in. I need to know more about what's happening. I need to go to school. I feel that part of my life has not been satisfied for a while.

Mothers need contact with their peers as much as monkeys and babies do, and a baby's new interest in her peers is often paralleled by her mother's renewed interest in friends. Unlike the seeking-out of other mothers of infants that occurred a few months before, the friends now sought are those who can share adult interests, new or revived. Lunch dates are made with former coworkers; friendships are struck that revolve about new interests and occupations.

Carol, who had spoken of her feeling that she was missing something from her children and who was spending more time with her older son, was also looking for something more:

~~ I decided that I wanted to take a carpentry course. I had a chance to rejoin my women's group and a chance to do some political work, and I decided to be selfish. I find that my work is so incredibly cerebral that I have to do something else. I even started baking bread.

The women who were having the greatest difficulty at this stage were those who had given up jobs or careers or study with only indefinite plans to return. Those who resumed work earlier, those who intended to return to a specific job on a particular date, and those who had decided to stay home for a year or more seemed able to cope with the tasks they faced and to make the changes that they all felt were necessary. The woman who knows exactly when she must return to work has usually planned in advance for child care. Some had made those arrangements, in fact, before their babies were born.

Women who were returning to work at six or seven months usually felt it was a good time to do so, unlike those who had had to leave their babies in the middle of the period of symbiotic closeness and found it a painful wrench. Many of those who were able to take the six-month moratorium felt that the situation was close to ideal. They got their rest, established their relationships with their babies, and saw them into the first phase of budding independence before going out themselves. Women who have to find jobs, to explore the possibilities for child care in their communities, to recognize and adjust to their babies' burgeoning sense of self and separateness, all with the usual minimum of social support available to mothers, are in a most difficult position. They are doing everything from scratch, and none of it is easy.

After six months the issue of money began to arise, especially among the nonworking mothers. During the moratorium even those who had always earned and spent their own money often seemed to feel that caring for the baby was enough. They had little need for their own money and few mixed feelings about spending their husbands'. The women who had the most traditional expectations wrote checks on the joint checking account without apparent compunctions, even though they made no direct contribution to it. A few, like Shirley, had had the foresight to put something aside and continued to use their own money for personal expenses. The women who had the greatest conflict about money seemed to be those who had been contributing substantial portions of the family income and expected to do so again in the future, but who found themselves, perhaps for the first time in their adult lives, financially dependent. Sarah was one of these.

～ I have no problem spending money for food, for things for the house, or for Jacob, but I can't spend money on myself. I can't bring myself to buy the smallest thing — a lipstick. I go in and I look at the lipsticks, and I know exactly what color I want and which one I would buy, if it was my money. It's like being on the dole. You're afraid someone's going to come along and accuse you of squandering their money.

At this point, too, money may become a family issue. The realization eventually sinks in that everything has become more expensive. Not only does the baby have to be fed and clothed — which has usually been anticipated, even if it was not sensibly provided for — but the apportioning of money also causes strains. The woman like Rosemary who decides that going back to school is the right thing for her to do may be forced to face the fact that the family income will simply not stretch to cover tuition and child care, especially if her own income is going to be reduced. Few couples seem to face in advance the constriction that results when three people have to live on one income. Some husbands are proud to be able to be the sole provider and feel strongly (sometimes more strongly than their wives) that their wives should not work while the children are small. Other men resent the lost income and become angry at wives who spend "his" money "frivolously."

The woman who cannot manage to organize her transition into the adult world at this point may express her difficulties through a period of depression and morbid preoccupation, or through projection of her frustrated desires onto the baby or someone else. Sarah, who several months earlier had told me about being overcome with rage and taking it out on the baby, was having a different kind of difficulty by the time Jacob was six-and-a-half months old. She had decided before he was born that she would give up teaching for a few years while she raised him (and, she thought, possibly another baby or two as well). Sarah welcomed Jacob's new developments and expressed no second thoughts about her decision to be a full-time mother.

∽ I think I give him a lot of love and attention without resenting it. I'm able to share and take enjoyment in a lot of things he's done — a lot of his new discoveries. I realize that I really enjoy playing with him.

When we talked, however, Sarah seemed a little bit flat, a little low-keyed. Sarah and I had a couple of mutual friends, and I knew that she had a reputation for vivacity, so I asked directly if she was feeling depressed.

∽ Yes. It has a lot to do with my feeling about having him, about staying home with him, being with him and somehow feeling like a lot of my days are purposeless, except for giving to him. I'm getting *something* back for that, but before I would go to school, and I would teach a class and feel like I was imparting knowledge to the students, or that at least I was doing something that had a greater meaning beyond myself and my own little world.

Sarah turned out to be rather perceptive about her state of mind and had followed the course of her feelings about herself rather closely:

∽ Since I've had Jacob, something has happened in the last month or so that didn't happen in the first few months that I had him (and this is related to my feeling about my work). I've had a lot of fears about my own mor-

tality; for the first time, it's really come to the fore that
I'm going to die some day. Since having him, all of a sudden
I'm terrified, having all these fantasies and fears about it,
as if somehow I'm going to die, and I haven't done anything
meaningful. What was the purpose of my life? I worry about
myself and my work, all intertwined. Watching him grow
and change — as he grows, my own life is ending somehow. I feel like I wouldn't have this feeling, if I didn't have
him.

Sarah seemed to be in mourning for a major portion of her
adult identity and saw its loss as her own death. One interview
study of women in pregnancy and the early postpartum weeks
found that "there was a considerable amount of grief work as
old roles were discarded — bride, schoolgirl, career woman."
While Sarah was further along in the motherhood process than
the women in this study, she too was doing "grief work," as
were the women who were mourning the loss of their prepregnant bodies and their prematernal sexuality.

Women who are frustrated in their adult strivings, who find
that, because of the demands of motherhood, they cannot fulfill
needs and goals of their own, may project their longings into
the infant. The need doesn't necessarily have to do with a career.
A woman may find no time for some recreation that was important to her, or find that she cannot muster the concentrated
attention required to pursue some occupation at home. I can
remember a neighbor — an artist — who became terribly depressed over her inability to paint at home as she had always
done. I can remember wondering why she was having such
difficulty, since she had a studio set up in her apartment and
up to four "free" hours a day, while her baby napped. What I
did not understand, being then childless, was that three or four
hours, one unpredictable part in the morning and the other in
the afternoon, do not allow for much continuity or concentration.

Elaine, the woman who had just resigned from her nursing

job, had been unusually athletic before and through her pregnancy, but she had not taken up any of her games since her son was born.

〜 The thing I miss most is sports — tennis, and we used to play touch football every weekend. I don't seem to have the time to get into shape. The few times I've managed to get someone to take care of Kenny so Dick and I could go out and play, I'm so out of shape it hasn't been much fun.

Kenny was a big baby, and an active one, though not abnormally so. Elaine insisted on his extraordinary mobility, agility, and determination.

〜 I can't leave him alone for a moment now. When he sets up a goal for himself, he can get there so fast. It looks like he's not doing anything, and then something catches his eye, and he's off. He's just incredibly active. The basic things are much easier now, but his activity level and his ability to move around — he's a problem in that respect. I leave him to get a glass of milk, and he's in the begonia, chewing away happily. I may have been gone all of ten seconds.

All this was said not in a tone of complaint, but with great pride. Elaine was delighted that her son's motor skills were developing a little precociously, and the development of his skills seemed to make up for the loss, however temporary, of her own.

Parents, of course, do project their needs, desires, and fears onto their children. The projections of the mothers in the early months were of fears — often fear of physical injury to the child. The fantasies about the babies, except for the very hostile ones mentioned earlier, were usually vague: "I want her to be smart or strong." In this later period, though, they seemed to have much more to do with the mother's own needs. Sarah, feeling isolated, bored, and helpless, but still able to articulate her need to be doing something independent of her son, said of the baby, "I really want Jacob to be independent of me. Nothing's worse than having a kid dependent on you." She was the woman who had reacted with unusual violence when her husband didn't arrive home to relieve her on schedule, an event which seemed to reinforce her recognition of her dependency on him. I felt, in talking with her about those incidents, that they may have been triggered by her resentment at being at her husband's mercy, at least as much as by fatigue and frustration. She was certainly aware of the difference between her husband's adult role and her own.

❧ Now I just stay home and all I have to talk about is gossip in the neighborhood, what I had for supper last night — very trivial kinds of things — or just talking about children. I realize I resent Peter a lot because he goes to work and gets to see people and talk about more interesting things.

Sarah and Elaine, and nearly all the other women were talking, not simply about taking up new or old activities, but about establishing or reestablishing roles which were important to their sense of identity as adults. A sense of continuity — I am the person to whom my past happened — is necessary to a person's sense of identity, but it is not sufficient in itself. Part of our sense of identity is gained from the recognition of ourselves by others. The sense that "I am a mother" comes from the baby's recognition of me in that role. But the sense that "I am an adult" depends upon recognition by others in the family or the community that I can fill the roles expected of an adult.

Sarah's lament that she had only trivial things to talk about would probably have sounded bizarre to a woman fifty years ago, for whom motherhood was the key to adulthood. Certainly it is clear from both history and novels of the nineteenth century that childless women — the barren, the spinster, the maiden aunt — were usually considered objects of pity and often of ridicule. The equation of motherhood with adulthood may be most common in societies where women do not engage in productive work (and so we see it most clearly in the Victorian middle and upper classes, where, until a woman had children, she usually had no household of any great size or complexity to manage).

While our society denies equal opportunity and equal pay to women in most fields and makes the management of motherhood and a job an almost superhuman task, we no longer seem to accord adult status to a woman simply because she has become a mother. On the contrary, many women who decide to stay at home to take care of their children, like Sarah, feel denigrated and seem defensive about their decision. Women in some subcultures, and especially in some ethnic enclaves, do not seem to suffer this particular problem. But for the middle class and a good portion of the working class as well, "just a mother" and "just a housewife" are not quite the equivalent of a real grown-up woman.

The devaluing of motherhood as an adult role arises, as Carol Gilligan has pointed out in *In a Different Voice: Psychological Theory and Woman's Development*, from the equation in psychology of "the qualities necessary for adulthood — the capacity for autonomous thinking, clear decision-making, and responsible action — . . . with masculinity." These qualities, among many others, are certainly necessary for the kind of mothering that most women expect of themselves, but because they are expressed in the context of relationships and not in the context of work, they become nearly invisible. "These stereotypes," Gilligan writes, "reflect a conception of adulthood that is itself out of balance, favoring the separateness of the individual self over connection to others, and leaning more toward an autonomous life of work than toward the interdependence of love and care." If maturity is the equivalent of masculinity, then femininity (and that uniquely feminine role, motherhood) must, by definition, be equivalent to immaturity.

There are deeper reasons for this devaluation of mothering, of course, and they have been explored and eloquently explained by Nancy Chodorow, in *The Reproduction of Mothering*, and by Dorothy Dinnerstein, in *The Mermaid and the Minotaur*. Although each writer comes to her subject from a different angle, they do agree that some of the adult (and specifically male adult) denigration of mothering and mothers is an attempt on the part of the now grown-up infant to obliterate the overwhelming power that the mother has over the infant.

Mothers, like everyone else, internalize these beliefs to some degree, so mothering for many women feels antithetical to real adulthood. The activities these women begin to take up in the sixth and seventh months do much more than fill time and offer occupation. They allow a mother to see herself in the role of *doing* whatever it is, of *being* the person who does it. To lose those roles and the recognition she achieves for them can easily leave a woman feeling like she is "just a mother," a complaint heard for the first time around this stage.

The complex of roles that a person plays in the world gives a context for the sense of internal continuity that forms the core of her identity. As she begins to remember and restore who she was, how she felt, how she looked, a woman must also restore that context. For the woman who has decided to put aside work or career, temporarily or permanently, this means finding some substitute for it, which will allow her to feel more competent and interesting (to herself and others), more than "just a mother." Learning to make pottery or bake bread can fill this need for a while, although for most women activities like these will have to become more than minor pastimes if they are to serve their real purpose of enlarging her sense of self.

The context of a woman's identity has of course been enlarged by the role of mother. While a woman will probably not have to get used to being called "Susie's mother" until Susie has playmates who can talk, the mother role, which has been of singular importance during its formative stage over the past few months, is now added indelibly to whatever other roles the woman may have. It is the reestablishment of those other roles that is the primary personal task of this period, as the realization of the role of mother was the primary task of the symbiotic phase. The integration of mother with the other roles is yet to come.

Being a mother in our culture implies taking responsibility. Every woman I interviewed understood that without ever having to be told. To be a *good* mother, a woman must love her child, but simply to *be* the child's mother she need only assume responsibility for that child and all its behavior and feelings, its failures and accomplishments. The responsibilities when the baby is six or seven months old still have to do primarily with caretaking. But even when there was someone else who did some of the actual caretaking work (even *most* of the actual work), there was never any question as to whose job it actually was, who was in charge, who was ultimately going to be held to account.

I never met a couple in which, for instance, the man had made a unilateral decision about who would be hired as a babysitter, no matter how great his involvement with the baby. In a few families, the man had interviewed prospective help with his wife, and the decision was made jointly, but in the vast majority of cases the decision was ultimately the woman's. As one mother put it, "I make the child-care arrangements because *I'm* the one who needs them. *I'm* the one who would be home otherwise."

In most households, if the sitter doesn't show up, if the child of the woman who cares for the baby is sick, or if the day-care center is closed for a holiday, it is almost invariably the mother who stays home, putting aside whatever else she may have to do and assuming her primary responsibility.

Another curious phenomenon, and one taken for granted by nearly everyone, is that the cost of child care is always computed out of the mother's wages. The assumption is again that the child is hers, that she is the one who needs child care, and that she is the one who should pay for it. A number of women, in fact, said that they could not go back to work (although they wanted the company and satisfaction of a job) because "by the time you pay the taxes and the sitter, there's nothing left." Mother is also the one who monitors the baby's development, who is expected to know when the baby requires immunizations and that if the baby is fussy one day it is because she is teething. She knows, as Rosemary said,

> ~ . . . every idiosyncrasy the baby has. I know exactly his measurement for formula and exactly how much he gets and what he gets at what time and what he gets in between. I know all that. Mike [her husband] doesn't know all that. He has stayed with Anthony on several occasions, and I had to write it down because that's not something he knows as I know it. I don't have to write it down for me.

There were many couples who shared a good deal of the work involved in having an infant, but even among most of these, as Shirley said,

> ~ No matter how much a man shares in the raising of the child, *you* do all the mental machinations.

By the time the baby is six months old a mother understands this kind of responsibility. She is responsible not only for the baby's care, but for the baby's safety and for the baby's development. She knows that if something goes wrong, whether she is present or not, it will have been her fault. If she was there when the accident took place, she should have prevented it; if she was *not* there, she should have been. She also knows that if the baby doesn't develop properly — if she doesn't learn things when she should — the mother will probably be held to blame.

One woman whose five-year-old daughter seemed to be mildly retarded said, "I think she's a little slow and she's bad-tempered. I'm sure it's because she was born right after her brother, and I never spent enough time with her. I had two of them in diapers, and I just never paid much attention to her." The little girl's problems, whatever they were, might just as well have resulted from her mother's chain-smoking throughout pregnancy, a forceps delivery, or poor nutrition in infancy, among a host of possibilities. Her mother, however, believed that it was her own inadequate mothering that was to blame.

Mothers are well aware that mothering is a job, and a full-time one at that. The job is done, by the sixth and seventh months, with some competence and usually a degree of pleasure. The tasks are better defined and so is the time spent. The hours and hours of holding and gazing and cooing are replaced by periods of play, caretaking, and outings. While these activities can be consuming, the mother usually has more time for contemplation and more time to spend on herself. The paradox of a twenty-four-hour job that still leaves time for doing or wishing to do other things has its effect on a woman's desire to repeat the experience of childbearing.

At every interview I asked each woman whether she wanted more children, and when. At first I was surprised to hear the mother of a two- or three-month-old baby say, as Rachel did:

> I'd like to get pregnant again *today.* I really want a big family. I guess realistically, I'd like to get pregnant again in a year.

Shirley, when her baby was scarcely three months old, said:

> She's so terrific. I'm all set to go again and have another, just to see what it looks like.

These women — and the rest echoed their sentiments — had achieved something during symbiosis which meant motherhood to them. The closeness with the baby and the ease and intimacy of a well-established symbiotic relationship made having another feel very attractive to them. It seemed easy, too, because they had no other very pressing demands. Their husbands were not, at that time, terribly demanding of their time and attention. No woman who said that she wanted another child right away was back at a job, and most were first-time mothers. They were in the moratorium, and they were enjoying it.

By six months they and their babies faced a more complicated situation. With only very few exceptions the mothers were engaged in pulling together the strands of their adult lives. The baby was for many more fun, but also more separate — a whole person to be considered and cared for, no longer a part of oneself. Rachel, back at work part-time, had changed her mind:

〜 Now that I'm settled in this schedule, I want to keep at it for a while and increase my hours slowly. I love my work. Maybe when Matthew's three, I'll think about another, but I know I'm not ready now. I had a pregnancy scare last week. It was a real scare. I just couldn't face another child now.

Rachel didn't seem to remember her earlier plan to have a second child within two years, and Shirley, who had been "ready" to have her second within the year, said when Patty was six months old:

〜 I want to have another one when they're three years apart. But you ask yourself, "How could I possibly love another child as much as I love this one, or get one that's as perfect, as pretty, as sociable?" But other people have more than one, so all right, but not now.

As the baby becomes a more and more individuated person, her mother thinks not just of continuing to be a mother, but of being a mother again to another, *different* person, and she worries more, as Shirley did, about who that person might be. Rosemary, who had decided to finish college, when asked if she wanted another child, said:

〜 Up to about a month or two ago, I was saying yes. I really do, but it's really hard. It's hard in terms of the things we have to get done. I guess when Anthony's three or four. I want to wait until he's walking around a lot and can understand it. Some people have them right away —

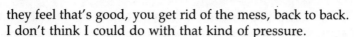

they feel that's good, you get rid of the mess, back to back. I don't think I could do with that kind of pressure.

Some women who had said earlier that they were actually considering having another child right away now explained their decision to wait by invoking the feelings of the older child. In this, of course, they find themselves in agreement with many child psychologists, who believe that sibling rivalry will not be so intense if the children are at least three years apart. For those who believe that sibling rivalry is something to be minimized, if not avoided altogether, this argument carries a good deal of weight. Some of the experts, however, especially the psychoanalysts, believe that sibling rivalry is a good and necessary part of growing up. Their primary argument is that it strengthens character and prepares the child for the real world.

For some mothers, the rationale for delaying having another child had to do with their sense that the family needed time to adjust to its new configuration. Sarah, in spite of her frustration at being home with the baby, was willing to consider having another, but was realistic about the strains it might put on her family.

 ⌒ Peter and I have been together for five years, and before we had Jake, we had hit a certain equilibrium with each other and resolved a lot of problems. Since Jake's been born, a lot of things have been coming up, and we realize there are lots of other problems to deal with. There's a really good feeling in being a family and doing things together, but we have to hit that equilibrium first, before we change the shape of the family again.

The need to establish equilibrium might be felt more by couples who had lived together, childless, for several years before having their first child. For them, the decision to have a child had usually been made only after much consideration, and sometimes hesitation. In retrospect they reported more doubts about *when* to have a baby than about whether to have one at

all. Elaine and her husband, however, had been altogether ambivalent about having a child. Her pregnancy was unplanned,
and she had left open the possibility of an abortion until the last
moment. When I asked if she thought of having more children,
she first literally hemmed and hawed, then finally said:

> ◈ Uh, well, yes, I guess, in my weaker moments. I don't
> know when, though. It's so hard for us to manage another
> way. When we got married, it was the two of us for seven
> years, and then we said, "What's going to happen when
> we have a kid?" We couldn't imagine. Then we started
> thinking about it, and we couldn't imagine having a kid,
> because the two of us had evolved our own life-style. Now
> we have Kenny, and it's just totally impossible for us to
> imagine having another child. It just seems like the whole
> unit got so coalesced. We thought it would never happen.

These women — most women — do not want to be mothers
again, so completely, so soon. While symbiosis holds them they
want to stay in it forever, but once it ends, as it had for these
women, life sets in and cannot be held away indefinitely. The
sense, that Elaine and Sarah expressed, of needing time to establish an equilibrium and to enjoy it reflects what most of the
women were saying in one way or another. The equilibrium has
to do with more than the family, though the state of the family
is important to the synthesis that is about to begin. More central
is the integration of the mother, who came to be through symbiosis, with the adult woman who is reasserting herself in the
sixth and seventh months. That integration is the job of the next
and last phase of the first nine months of motherhood.

CHAPTER 6

THE EIGHTH AND NINTH MONTHS
Together Again

1

THE NINE-MONTH-OLD BABY moves away from her mother, then back to her, and again away. As a mother and I sit talking, the baby wakes from her nap. The mother goes to get her. She brings her in, puts her down, and the baby's off. She is no longer content to sit at her mother's feet; she wants to be doing something on her own. She crawls across the room, rolls herself up to a sitting position, picks up a block in one hand, a second block in the other. For a few minutes, she is absorbed in her play, but often she glances over her shoulder at her mother. Soon, she crawls back to where her mother sits, plays briefly near her, then asks to be lifted to her lap, but she doesn't remain there long. She slides off, crawls to the coffee table, pulls herself to her feet and begins to walk around and around and around the table. Periodically she checks back to her mother, and from time to time she returns to her mother for what Margaret Mahler calls "refueling."

The baby is clearly aware that her mother is separate — that she is separate. The baby can be alone, but needs to touch base every once in a while. Mahler calls this the "early practicing period." (The "practicing period proper" arrives when the baby begins to walk.) Most of the baby's energies are invested in practicing and perfecting her motor skills, especially the large motor skills of crawling and cruising, and she spends hours each day at these activities.

By the time a baby passes seven months her ability to move about is accompanied by a number of other accomplishments — signs of her accelerating motor development, of her new perceptual abilities, and of the great psychological changes underway. Sitting up unaided is no longer an accomplishment; it is something she does without thinking much about it. She gets from place to place by one or another means, with more or less speed, but always with great purpose and attention to her goal. She practices standing, often even in the middle of the night, and by eight months she probably cruises along, holding onto a table or other furniture or to the hand of a larger person. Her hands now work with precision; tiny objects can be grasped and are usually placed directly into her mouth. No longer does she poke herself in the eye or inadvertently stick the rattle in her ear. Her aim is exact.

The baby will now search for an object that she has seen hidden, no longer believing (as she apparently did a month or so earlier) that once she cannot see it, it no longer exists. Her recognition that something she cannot see is nonetheless still where it was is called *object permanence*. It is believed to affect not only her response when her bottle is hidden under a blanket, but also her reaction when her mother leaves the room. Where earlier she might sit, quietly or crying, looking toward the door through which her mother disappeared, she is now likely to follow her and to search until she finds her.

The baby's ability to imitate (in a much more conscious and complex manner than that of a newborn imitating a stuck-out tongue) and her pleasure in doing so is another sign of psychological development. It signals that she knows she is separate, but enough like those around her to try to do many of the same things they do. Her mimicry may now begin to extend to language, as she learns to control and repeat some of the sounds she has been babbling, apparently randomly, for months.

While a good many people, and even some mothers, seem to be able to ignore the infant's development in the first six months, there is no way to ignore what is going on now. Pamela, the mother of an eight-and-a-half-month-old son, gave a typical account.

> ✌ He's crawling, he's standing, he's cruising. He can pick up chairs with two fingers. He's imitating language — not terribly accurately — but he's saying "gaga" for "bye-bye." We see his mouth going, and he's trying to learn. He's very fast. He likes to stand and hold on with one hand. Eventually, of course, if he lets go, he'll go straight down. He's into picking up little pieces of lint from the carpet.

The new ability to crawl is typically employed by the baby to crawl away, particularly from anyone who might try to restrain her. Faced with a flight of stairs, most will go straight up with great speed and agility. Getting down is a different matter, and babies this age must be taught by example how to back down, lest they fall. Many must be carried down the stairs, still unable to coordinate the descent. And many, once carried down, will head directly back up, over and over again. The drive to move is intense, and it can become difficult, as it did for Ellen, to perform even the most routine chores with the baby:

> ✌ He doesn't want to stop for anything. It's very hard putting diapers on him. Even when he stands, he twists around and grabs my hair. He's really a handful.

Very much in keeping with their resistance to being kept still and their new sense of independence, most babies by nine months (or very shortly thereafter) will try to wean themselves from the breast. Whether the rebellion against the breast is simply a sign of the baby's dislike of being held in the nursing position, or is a sign of her need for psychological distance from her mother, the results are clear. Most mothers, if they continue to breastfeed past this age, have to acknowledge that it is done as much to satisfy themselves as it is to fulfill any need of the baby's.

By the time a baby reaches six months, the benefit of the mother's immunities diminishes (most babies are being immunized by their doctors by this age, anyway), and most babies are eating some variety of solid foods and formula or cow's milk to meet their nutritional requirements. There is no apparent psychological benefit in breastfeeding, whether it is done for a few weeks or a few years, that anyone has been able to distinguish. (It also seems to be the case that if a mother misses or ignores the baby's desire to wean at this stage and continues to breastfeed, it becomes much more difficult to wean the baby at a later stage. Mothers who have insisted that their babies continue to nurse past a year sometimes find that the child of two or three or four, now vocal and mobile, refuses rather violently to be weaned once and for all.)

Cultures which practice prolonged breastfeeding — sometimes until the child is three or four — do so for a variety of reasons. Where the overall diet is poor and the water supply is not reliably clean, breast milk provides clear health benefits to the growing baby. As long as the child is being nursed frequently, breastfeeding acts as a contraceptive for the mother. In the absence of more reliable methods, breastfeeding allows a reasonable spacing of children. Nursing only three or four times a day, however, provides little contraceptive effect, and so does not make a dependable method for most of us.

When a baby is offered nothing but the breast, there is probably less motivation for her to reject it. For our babies, though, who by the age of eight or nine months are usually eating three meals a day, it becomes very difficult to maintain an interest in nursing. One mother who was still nursing her baby early in the morning and late at night commented, "It's still a comforting thing for us both, but I have a feeling it's going to come to an end soon, because it's already not like it was."

Another, who had been advised by her pediatrician that she would be wise to continue to breastfeed until the baby was a year old, because of a strong family history of allergies, said when the baby was almost nine months old:

❧ Now I'm sure if Pat had his druthers, he would like to be weaned, but my doctor would like him not to go on whole milk for a year, so I'm determined to nurse him for a year. He just does it to do me a favor. He wakes up in the morning, and he'd rather have his food. It's for me, and I keep at it.

It seems that relatively few women wean their babies without some mixed feelings. There is no mystery here. The strong physical and emotional tie between a mother and her infant is invariably symbolized by the baby at the breast, and weaning seems to be universally understood as a loosening, or at least a change in the quality of that tie. Whole schools of psychology are founded on this understanding, and at whatever age weaning occurs, mothers know what is going on. When Daniel was just nine months old, Ellen described her feelings about breast-feeding him:

❧ I have a feeling he could give it up real easily. I don't think my breasts will suffer; I have so little milk anyway. I never feel that full really. I feel like I've weaned him from me in some way, but I haven't. It seems really quite difficult for me to give it up, although on the other hand, I'm really wanting to. I'm just not sure that there's some *not* wanting to make it final.

By nine months many mothers find that the effort required to keep the baby's attention (and mouth, for that matter) on the breast is not worth the effort. The babies can hold the bottle very competently by this age (some can even drink efficiently from a cup), but even those who cannot or will not hold the bottle themselves seem to prefer it to the breast. They all like to be fed in a sitting position, rather than in the supine position that nursing requires. They can feed themselves with their fingers, by now, although most are still laughably clumsy with a spoon. Many babies prefer to feed themselves almost entirely, and their ability to feed themselves adequately can solve many of the feeding problems that arise at this time. The drive for independence can also be seen in some babies' resistance to being fed by their mothers in particular. Ellen was especially perceptive about the reasons for her difficulty in feeding Daniel, though her insight was not quite sufficient to alleviate the problem entirely.

~ He's much more resistant to eating with me than with Ed [her husband] or Dee [his sitter]. His mealtimes have become a struggle, and I get crazy around that. I think I want to force him to eat. I have to really struggle with myself to say the hell with it, he doesn't have to eat. I sit there feeling my whole body get tense, while he sits looking away when I put the spoon up to his face. It's not because he's not hungry, because then, after he wouldn't eat this morning, he had practically eight ounces of milk, and he just guzzled it down. He just didn't want to be fed. That was a passive thing. He wanted to be more active. It's not a rational thing. It has to do with rejecting me.

Around nine months most of the mothers perceived, as Ellen did, a change in the baby's relationship to them. Not all felt rejected. Some could best be described as relieved by the new developments — the babies had acquired a new sense of independence. That is not to say at all that they no longer needed their mothers or regularly expressed that need, but the quality of the need had changed. Now they needed someone to help them into the world, teach them things, and show them things, rather than only sheltering them and ministering to them. And they needed someone to allow them to explore on their own. The babies recognized themselves as separate, and they began to experiment with separateness and separation.

Ellen said:

~ One of the things he's gotten into in a big way is feeding me things. Not just food, but everything. He'll put a toy in his mouth, and then give it to me and want me to put it in my mouth. That feels like a part of the whole separation process.

The baby's earlier idea that she and her mother were one is being replaced by something much more complicated. She is beginning to see herself, not as identical with her mother as she did in symbiosis, but identifying with her mother and others around her. She is separate, but like them. She can do some of the things that they can, and she seems now to realize that she can learn to do more. By making his mother imitate him, Daniel confirms for himself that they are much alike, and perhaps recaptures some feeling that he can make his mother do things, the feeling he had when he was three months old and thought that he made the breast appear when he felt hungry and cried.

The baby's growing sense of herself as an individual is matched by her increasing individuality. *The First Twelve Months of Life*, a book on infant development, states the situation succinctly in the chapter on the baby's ninth month:

> Differences among babies will be more pronounced than they were during the first six months of life, when the baby's brain and nervous system were changing more dramatically and his reflexes were more in control of his movements.

While anyone can confidently predict that a baby will smile by six or seven weeks, it cannot be as confidently said, for instance, that they will all crawl by nine months. They are all, or virtually all, sitting by this age, but there are many who are doing little else, in terms of large muscle development. Some, on the other hand, are nearly ready to walk, and a very few already can. Some can stand without support; many can walk holding onto the furniture or someone else's hand. Most, though not all, crawl by this age or have some way of getting around, though it may be only by bouncing along on the backside.

As the large and small muscle skills develop, as they do very quickly in this period, the baby's personality emerges more distinctly. Families are aware of the baby's personality from a very early age, though there can be surprises — the irritable and colicky newborn who turns out to be a charming and even-tempered baby; the apparently placid infant who, once able to move, seems unable to stop. By the time the baby is eight or nine months old, there are usually qualities about her, though they may be apparent only to those very close, that will remain more or less consistent for a long time to come. That is not to say that a baby who takes a long time to learn to sit or walk or handle a spoon comfortably won't later turn out to be extremely quick at developing social or intellectual skills, but the style of learning can often be perceived by an interested observer as early as eight or nine months.

Some babies from early on will plunge into a new task or situation, get fully involved, and seem to figure out the details from the inside. Others will remain on the sidelines a little longer, watching, figuring out what is going on before entering in themselves. Some will always use their hands first; others will use their eyes or their ears. Some will show a boldness that they never lose, though at some stages that boldness will look like recklessness and at others like courageous determination. Others are shy or good-natured or easily frustrated. Most mothers, by the time their babies reach this age, are able to give a fairly rounded, objective, and complex picture of the baby when asked.

2

Most of the mothers I interviewed were delighted with their babies' emerging skills and their increasingly well-defined personalities. The babies, able to move around, were better able to amuse themselves and usually left their mothers more time to themselves. Routines were well established. When they were not — when the disorganization typical of the symbiotic phase persisted this long, and a woman still couldn't find the time to do anything, couldn't establish or maintain a schedule — there usually seemed to be more serious underlying problems.

Terry was twenty-one. She had worked at a clerical job until shortly before her baby was born. She believed that it was best for mothers to stay home until their children were of school age, and she had no plans to return to outside work. Her son, at the time of the interview, was nine months old. One characteristic of this period is that a woman has usually regained her ability to analyze and manage relationships within the family, which, no matter what else she may do, is one of her key functions in the contemporary family. Terry was unable to analyze, or even to describe in any detail, her relationships with her husband and her son.

When I first saw Terry at four months, she seemed swallowed in a symbiotic relationship with the baby, from which she seemed to derive no pleasure at all. The baby took up all her time and attention. "But," she complained, "he doesn't do any tricks yet." Her life was entirely taken up with trying to get him onto a schedule, with keeping him clean, keeping him quiet. She said that she couldn't wait for him to grow up. He didn't eat neatly, didn't nap at the same time every day, and he cried. At nine months, Terry said:

∽ I'm constantly doing something for the baby. It's changing him, or feeding him, or holding him, or whatever, so it's constantly with him. Everything is with him; nothing is alone. No more doing the nails. No time for the hair. That's the worst of it — no time for myself. He goes to sleep, but then there's things to do when he's sleeping, like the laundry, I do at night, so it's really hard getting out.

Her husband was willing to stay with the baby if Terry wanted to visit a friend or go out for coffee in the evening, but she had done so only a very few times.

∽ I've been feeling lately that I'm ready for a break-down. I told him that. I know I'm going crazy because it's too much. I don't leave him [the baby] with anyone. It's my fault that I don't leave him with anyone. I can get a baby-sitter. Not that I have a lot of money to spend on a babysitter, but I can do it once in a while — get a babysitter and go out. But I'm afraid to leave him with anyone. I'm afraid that if I'm not here, if there's a sitter, that something'll go wrong. I get nervous, so I don't leave him.

She said of the baby, who spent much of his waking time in a playpen:

~✓ I don't like to keep him confined. I don't want to keep him like a prisoner or anything, but he's all over everything. He goes to the fishtank, he goes over to the television, he goes to the wrought iron chairs, he's all over everything. And he's gotten hurt. Quite a number of times. But I guess that's the only way they learn, when they fall and get hurt. I know when he's going to get hurt, and I let it happen. Not because I want him to get hurt, but because he's got to learn how not to get hurt, and I feel they learn it by getting hurt. And they'll get hurt the first time, and the second time, and maybe even four or five times, but then they'll stop.

She couldn't leave him with her parents in the evening for fear he'd wake up. She couldn't take him with her to visit her old office, for fear that "this kid is going to start screaming in the middle of the bus, or start screaming in the middle of the office, or something. So I don't do it."

She sounded like many of the mothers of two-month-old babies, for whom the logistics of getting out of the house were so overwhelming. But there were few other mothers who could not manage to navigate the world with a nine-month-old. The reasons for the mothers' inability to get out with the babies (and for their reluctance to leave them with anyone else) when the babies were a month or two months old still seemed to hold for Terry; her attachment to the baby seemed extremely tenuous.

(In the course of a very long interview, she referred to him as "him" or "this kid," and not once by his name.) Like the others earlier, she felt that if, because of her weak attachment, she couldn't trust herself with him, she certainly couldn't trust someone else. She bitterly resented the fact that her brother and sister-in-law had never offered to take the baby for a day or an evening, yet I suspected that, had they done so, Terry would have found some reason for being unable to leave the baby with them, as she was reluctant to leave him with her parents.

Terry's complaints about the baby's mobility were the only spontaneous comments she made about her son. Most mothers in our culture are proud of each new step the baby takes. When I asked Terry about the baby, her responses were brief and superficial, and she soon veered back to talking about herself: "He's good. He doesn't cry too much, and he plays by himself in the playpen for a couple of hours, so I can get something done."

I noticed that when he was not in the playpen he rarely approached his mother. The one time he did so, he crawled over to her and pulled himself up on her leg. She shooed him away, telling him to go and play with his toys. He looked distressed, but didn't cry and soon crawled away. Terry seemed stuck — not just stuck in the house, which she obviously was, but stuck at an earlier stage. She sounded like an amplified version of a woman with a five- or six-month-old, a woman whose attention was centered on herself, with very little left for the baby, but Terry, unlike most of the others, showed little prospect of change.

Although Terry was past her teens, she was in a way like the teenage mothers I interviewed. Most teenagers become pregnant by accident; they do not, contrary to myths about them, unconsciously want to be pregnant. Those who choose to keep and raise their babies do so because the social sanctions against doing so are much less stringent than they used to be. Teenagers often make good mothers to very young infants. They gain, from mothering a tiny, helpless creature, a feeling of power and competence that does not exist in any other area of their lives. But the moment the baby begins to show the least sign of autonomy, be it so simple as looking away or sitting up unaided, the young mother begins to feel, as one sixteen-year-old said of her six-month-old baby, that "he doesn't need me anymore."

Terry was left with nowhere to turn when the baby began to make his first independent moves. A woman's task at six months is to recapture her adult self, but Terry, like the teenagers, had very little adult self to begin with. When her son was four months old she had said, "I want to grow up with my baby." But a mother's job, if she is to be an adequate parent, requires that she *be* a grownup and able to mother a no-longer-helpless, rapidly developing baby. The very young mothers are not to be blamed for their own inadequacy. Alice Radosh, Coordinator of Adolescent Pregnancy and Parenting Services for the City of New York, where one-third of all babies are now born to unwed teenagers, said recently: "A baby needs a grown-up for a mother from six months on, and a fifteen-year-old can't be that; in fact, she shouldn't *have* to be that."

To do their own work of maturing, the teenaged mothers (and the no longer teenaged but still immature women, like Terry) had to turn away from their babies, once the babies were no longer such helpless infants. Such mothers simply didn't yet have the necessary resources to mother their babies. Several of them actually turned the babies over to their own mothers. The young mothers wanted a helpless being, with whom they could be all-giving and all-powerful. The baby's developing selfhood was a threat with which they were unready to cope.

Maxine was a woman with slightly different problems. Her daughter at nine months was a pretty, wiry, active baby who seemed particularly fussy. Asked what the baby was doing developmentally, Maxine said:

~ She sits and she crawls. She doesn't like to crawl — she'd rather walk with me holding her hands, because that way she can hang on to me. If she crawls, she has to go away from me, which she doesn't like to do too much.

This last was said with a note of pride. As we continued to talk, the baby continued to fuss. Maxine talked to her, presented her with toys, bounced her up and down, nursed her. They had no schedule, she said, except that imposed by a swimming class they took together once a week and a child development class to which she took the baby twice a week. At home, there was no real routine, because "If I have something to do, I won't put her down and let her cry. I'd rather do it when she's asleep or not do it at all."

Since the baby was born, Maxine had been out without her twice, both times for brief outings. On both occasions, the baby's father had stayed with her.

~ He loves to play with her, and they get along fine, but she still would rather be with me. She doesn't want to be out of my sight. If he's playing with her next to me, it's OK, but if he takes her out of the room, she gets upset. She really is crazy about him, it's just that she'd rather have me holding her.

Maxine did indeed hold the baby *all* the time, and the baby fussed continuously. When I had been there for about an hour, the telephone rang. Maxine leaned to get it, and in doing so, momentarily released her hold on the baby. In a flash, the baby walked unsteadily but barely touching the sofa back for support, over to me and settled herself in my lap. For the first time since I had arrived, she was quiet.

For the mother of a nine-month-old, Maxine had an unusual view of her responsibilities.

~ I feel bad sometimes when I feel like I'm not figuring out what she wants. It seems to take time sometimes to figure out what they want, and I feel bad about that. Maybe

I'm holding her sometimes, and I'm not really concentrating on her and talking to someone or talking on the phone, and all of a sudden I realize she wanted to do something.

The baby's fussing did seem unfocused, and her signals were not at all clear. They didn't have to be. She knew that her mother would take all the time necessary to find out what it was she wanted. Maxine spent her entire day concentrating on the baby. When I asked what she did for herself, she seemed unable to understand the question.

~ For myself? Doing for myself? I don't know. It just draws a blank. I don't know. What do I do for myself? Like what?

I explained that I meant interests pursued on her own, time for herself, taking care of herself, indulging herself. "Well," she finally responded, "I eat."

When the babies reach nine months, most mothers can give a fairly sophisticated analysis of the child, her personality, her skills. Maxine, in spite of her obsession with the baby, could not do so at all. She was simply too close to the baby to have any perspective. She referred to the baby by name only once, and when she spoke to her, addressed her as "Mama's little girl," "Mama's little sugarbun," or some such possessive endearment. The only reading matter in her apartment were several books on childrearing and a few copies of *Mothering* magazine. The baby slept with her, in spite of the resentment of the baby's father (they were not married). I asked how long she planned to continue breastfeeding. "As long as she wants to," Maxine replied. "I could never deny her that."

There was a photograph in the room where we sat of a young woman who bore a slight facial resemblance to Maxine. She had, she told me, a younger sister, but their relationship was filled with conflict and rivalry, and it seemed unlikely that the picture was one of her sister. Reaching for discretion, I indicated it and asked, "When was that taken?" "Just before I got pregnant," was the reply. I expected the answer, but was nonetheless shocked by it. The woman in the picture was forty or fifty pounds thinner than the one who sat before me, but the difference was more than physical. The woman in the photograph looked ten years younger and exuded a sense of vitality and energy that was hard to reconcile with the placid, matronly woman in the room.

Maxine looked like a woman still in a very bad version of symbiosis, and of course, that is precisely what she was. She was trying to prolong the symbiotic attachment — trying to hold the baby long after it made any sense at all for her to do so. The baby, who took the first opportunity to escape her mother's grasp, who did, in fact, exactly what her mother said she did not like to do — move *away* from her — was desperate to get out of her mother's clutches.

Margaret Mahler theorizes that babies who walk very early do so in cases exactly like this. The mother tries to prolong symbiosis, will not let the baby turn away from her and begin to move, discourages every sign of independence. And the baby, in response, walks away at the earliest opportunity. Even Maxine noticed that her daughter was nearly ready to walk unassisted. While Mahler believes that all babies take their first steps *away* from their mothers — a primary sign of independence and separateness — mothers can tell you that that is not the case. Most times, as Alice described the scene, "You say, 'Come, come, come,' and then suddenly, they do." But Maxine's daughter, I thought, would do precisely what Mahler predicted. This was a child looking for a way out.

The psychologist Sylvia Brody commented in a 1970 article that ". . . the self-sacrificing mother . . . appears figuratively in religious themes, and actually in social groups in which few nondomestic sublimations are available to married women. The 'selfless' mother was more familiar in a prefeminist era." Maxine did seem to have internalized the myth of the perfect mother, or of a certain kind of perfect mother, to the point that she was completely unable to release the baby or to recognize the baby's apparent need for a little bit of independence.

The literature on mothering that Maxine had chosen to read — the La Leche League handbook, called *The Womanly Art of Breastfeeding;* a book called *The Family Bed,* about the benefits of allowing a child to sleep with her mother until the child decides not to; and *Mothering* magazine — all advance a rather self-sacrificing style of mothering. La Leche counsels mothers to nurse their babies and children on demand, for as long as the child wants to continue. (In their publication *Breastfeeding and Working?* the mother of a one-year-old writes that, on weekends, she and her little girl "resume a normal relationship. Chrissie usually nurses about ten to fifteen times a day. . . .") La Leche, in all its literature, stresses the importance of the mother and her uninterrupted presence, as well as her willingness to nurse the child whenever and wherever, because it is only the mother who can adequately understand and meet all the child's needs. They suggest that a mother who feels that she must work for financial reasons consider moving to a smaller house, having her husband take a second job, going on welfare, or arranging with her creditors not to pay the bills on time.

Maxine had accepted that being a good mother meant responding immediately to every one of the baby's wishes. Frequent nursing, which is often unavoidable when a baby is two or three months old, can certainly make it difficult for a mother to establish any sort of schedule, for her baby or herself, and may leave her, as it did Maxine, in the disorganized state typical of symbiosis. There were more parallels to symbiosis than only this one, however: Maxine was striving desperately to continue the oneness of symbiosis, even after the baby had outgrown it, and to keep her daughter in a completely infantile state by treating her like an infant — never letting go and not recognizing or encouraging any signs of growth. There is no evidence whatsoever, of course, that the romantic and idealized Mother that

Maxine seemed to be trying to be is good for children, but the selfless (and suffocating) mother presented in the literature that Maxine had chosen to read clearly met some psychological needs of her own, even if it did not suit those of her baby.

3

During symbiosis the response to the baby's behavior is fairly predictable from one mother to the next. Almost any adult, but especially one who is in regular, close contact with the infant, will answer the baby's smiles with smiles of her own, the infant's coos and gurgles with imitations. With the reassertion of the adult personality that occurs in the sixth and seventh months, however, the mother responding to the older baby will show more individually characteristic behavior than she did earlier.

Where almost anyone will respond to the four-month-old's grimace with one similar, the mother of a nine-month-old who is crawling into danger may let her go, so that she can learn what not to do in the future; may grab her out of harm's way; may say, "No, no," to warn her; may distract her so that she'll go in another direction; or may remove the source of danger from the baby's path. A mother may respond to the game of "dropping the cup" by patiently picking it up and returning it to the baby time and time again; by ignoring the whole business, no matter how loudly the baby complains; or by removing the cup from the baby's sight, with confidence that the baby's memory is still short and that, within a minute or so, she will find something else to occupy her.

Babies are aware of separations from their regular caretakers well before eight months, although some begin showing more reaction as they get older. Shirley described an incident that took place when Patty was eight months old:

✒ For the first time, on Saturday, we went to a big party, and after several hours I wanted to go outside for a while, and she watched me walk out of the room, could see I was walking out the door, and she started to cry. I waved to her, and I said, "Bye, Patty," but I didn't go back. And I left. My husband was there, and she was fine as soon as I went through the door.

The baby's new awareness of separation is usually accompanied by a new response to strangers. This response has been called "stranger anxiety" or "eight-month anxiety," and is supposed to be characterized by fear of strangers and crying at the sight of someone new. Most of the women I interviewed said that their babies did not, in fact, cry at the sight of strangers, and in my personal experience this extreme reaction is most unusual, though the delighted smiles and reaching out at the sight of a new face that were so notable in the five-month-old are gone.

The reaction to strangers, which in reality ranges from no reaction at all to the classic screwing up the face and crying, seems to have to do with the baby's ability to distinguish the familiar face from the unfamiliar one. The baby who is accustomed to many different people, and who is generally confident of good treatment at the hands of whoever is with her, is not likely to express fear at the sight of someone new. She is, however, now able to recognize that someone is a stranger and to wait and see how that stranger behaves toward her.

Among the women I interviewed, Maxine and Terry were exceptional in having something approaching an exclusive relationship with their babies. In many households, the baby's father was involved to a considerable degree and participated regularly in at least some aspects of baby care. Some of the women, especially those in working-class families, had networks of family and friends on which they depended for some help with the baby, and who provided a variety of relationships for baby and mother. Some had mothers or aunts or sisters nearby; some had close neighbors with whom they occasionally or regularly left the baby. So it was, in fact, a very rare baby who did not have a regular experience of being with adults other than her mother.

There is a good deal of controversy concerning stranger anxiety. In experimental set-ups, in this country and in England, researchers have usually been able to demonstrate that some babies at some ages show negative responses to some people acting in some ways. But the age at which the negative reaction to strangers peaks has been reported as early as three months, while other investigators find that it peaks some time during the second year. A lot seems to depend on how the stranger acts: It is far easier to elicit a negative response if you approach abruptly, keep a straight face and bob your head up and down, or proceed to undress the baby and examine her. In general, in the experiments, the closer the investigator was able to approximate the normal behavior of a friendly stranger making a cautious approach to the infant, the less likely the negative response became.

The familiarity of the situation also affects the infant's response, and it is harder to get the baby to cry at the sight of a stranger in her own home than it is in the laboratory or the doctor's office. Culture also plays a role: One investigator reports that stranger anxiety seems not to occur in Japanese children. Rene Spitz placed the peak of stranger anxiety at eight months, and his finding has been generally accepted in the popular wisdom. He is nearly alone among the investigators, however, in finding that particular peak for stranger anxiety, so it is not terribly surprising that none of the women I interviewed reported strong negative reactions to strangers when the babies were eight months old. Since the very existence of the response is in question, we can probably view with some skepticism Spitz's construction that the presence of the response indicates the development of a specific attachment to the mother (which is violated by the sight of a stranger and causes the baby to react negatively).

When I asked Pamela about her eight-month-old son's response to strangers, she reported an incident that is somewhat illuminating:

> ❧ He has not really gone into stranger anxiety, which they're supposed to do, and a lot of them really don't. He did do it once with someone who looks a little bit like my sister, because I think he was trying to relate to her and then found out it was the wrong person. Then he burst into tears.

The baby, who easily perceives differences in appearance and behavior, is perhaps reacting to a violation of her expectations — to strangeness, not to strangers. The reaction of a baby at this age to the mother's leaving seems as variable as the response to strangers. John Bowlby, among others, believes that a baby's protest at her mother's departure is an indicator of the strength of the baby's attachment to her. Again, the studies on separation reaction rarely observe the baby in what would be a more or less normal setting for separation to occur. Few mothers, except in an experimental situation, simply put the baby down in a strange room with a strange person and leave. Even an adult might get a little suspicious being taken by a trusted companion to a strange place and left with a stranger without warning, explanation, or introduction. For a baby to start to cry under such circumstances seems perfectly reasonable, yet many separation experiments are conducted in just this way, and conclusions are drawn from their results.

It would make more sense for such an experiment to be conducted in the baby's home, observing the baby's behavior when she is left with a familiar and trusted person. Most babies, under these "normal" circumstances, will show their awareness of their mothers' departure. And most mothers make something of a ritual of leavetaking, including kisses and much waving and repeating of "bye-bye." It has, in fact, been argued that a baby who cries inconsolably at her mother's leaving is suffering from a less strong and secure attachment than the baby who can accept the separation with more equanimity. While there are exceptions, most babies accustom themselves rather quickly to regular separation from their mothers.

While many of the early infant studies were done with babies who were being raised in institutions (who do not, of course, represent a normal population), the more recent studies are generally done with babies and children of two-parent families, in which the father works and the mother stays home with the children. (This kind of bias in selection does not have to be deliberate. Mothers with outside jobs are usually not available during working hours to participate in experiments.) But as recent statistics show, this "typical" nuclear family is becoming more and more unusual and now represents only about 12 percent of U.S. households. Most of those who study infants have an implied, if not an explicit bias, against the mother who works outside the home, and even against the one who, for any reason, spends much less than all her time with the baby.

In Sylvia Brody's longitudinal study, *Patterns of Mothering*, one baby's developmental problems are attributed to her mother's desperation to return to her writing when the baby was only a few months old and, later, to her actually having done so. There is no hint that the obvious strains in this mother-baby relationship might have resulted from the frustrations of a woman who was better suited to part-time than to full-time mothering, or that the mother and baby might both have benefited had the mother had support for resuming work from her family, her community, and the investigators. A study published in 1963 found that well-adjusted children have mothers who are satisfied with their lives, whether or not the mother is working. The woman who is happy at home and the woman who is happy at work would then appear to have the same chance for having healthy, happy children.

In Margaret Mahler's study of development in the first years of life, the mothers who participated in the study are described as those who "were sufficiently interested in, and aware of, the rewards and problems of childrearing to want to remain with their young children." The inference one draws is that, first, the woman who does not remain with her young child is not interested and aware of the rewards and problems and, second, that she necessarily *chooses* to remain or not.

Neither is a safe assumption. Many women, well aware of the rewards and problems of childrearing, would rather not experience them all the time, or feel that they can better appreciate the rewards and cope with the problems if they have other occupations as well. The question of "choosing" to stay at home or to work outside is even trickier. Most women, like most men, work because they must, and the majority who return to jobs when their babies are very young usually do so from necessity. The salary is essential (this is especially true for single mothers), or the employer will grant only a few weeks' maternity leave, and they cannot afford to lose the job. Some women, too, as discussed in Chapter 5, feel that by staying home they are doing what is considered proper work only for idiots, and that for the sake of maintaining some self-respect, they must return to work promptly. Whether they return to work out of necessity or desire, most mothers nonetheless feel that they are violating a social norm and risking their children's mental health, as well. The mothers who returned to outside work at six or nine months suffered only slightly less from guilt and from its social reflection — the disapproval of family and community — than did those who returned at six weeks or three months.

When Molly was born in 1973 there was considerable support within my social circle for not making a great fuss over the fact that one had recently had a baby. Child care, even for infants, was available, not widely and seldom cheaply, but there were public and private day-care centers, especially in major cities, that accepted infants at one or two or three months of age. Women then were just beginning the battle for an equal place with men in the economy, and dropping out did not serve that struggle. Middle-class women who chose to stay home were often defensive about that decision.

Today the ideological pendulum has swung, and in the face of the evidence that more mothers of infants are in the workforce than were there ten or twelve years ago, the accepted wisdom is that mothers belong at home. Bowlby's books have recently been reissued, and his beliefs concerning the need for exclusive mothering gain currency in the writing of authorities such as Selma Fraiberg, in newspapers and popular magazines. Women who once wrote about their struggle to become whole, complex human beings now write about the pleasures of prolonged breastfeeding and the joy of teaching their daughters to make a proper pie crust. The romanticizing of motherhood and the instructions for making it a full-time job are reinforced by the dearth of group care for infants and the often prohibitive cost of individual care, the low pay for most women's jobs, and the lack of adequate paid maternity and paternity leave.

The denial of the demands and the rewards of mothering an infant, which led some women in the early 1970s to try to fit a baby into an already full life and to pretend that it was easy, has been replaced in the '80s by the promotion of motherhood as an adequate substitute for all the other aspects of the life of an adult woman. As women in the early '70s strove to achieve a balance that would include their children in their lives, many today are striving for a balance that includes themselves. Alison was a woman facing just this problem, when her daughter was nine months old:

〜〜 Even though I'm still home with her, I've kept on with the other parts of my life, but it hasn't been easy. I know what I need to do now. The problem is my husband, who wants *his* child to have a "real mother."

But the other side of the problem continues to exist for some. Joyce, a molecular biologist who had taken most of the first five months off to be home with her daughter (except for teaching one class and a limited amount of time in the laboratory), said:

> ~ I've always thought of myself as very work-oriented. My fantasy was that I'd run back to work and not feel torn. It's *not* that I feel torn — I feel she's in good hands — but I'd like to spend more time with her than just seeing her on weekends, which is almost what happens when I work full-time and come home at six.

Joyce did, of course, see the baby every evening for about two hours; "just seeing her on weekends" was more an expression of anxiety than of reality. For the woman who returns to a job, whether the baby is six weeks or six months or a year old, the most pressing problem is child care. A few have dependable relatives who care for the baby for no or relatively little pay. The rest face a choice among costly and often not entirely satisfactory alternatives. Many of the babies, by the time they reach eight or nine months, have been through at least one change in child-care arrangements. A sitter might be found to be irresponsible or too controlling, a group care arrangement too lax or too busy for the particular infant. Individual sitters and unlicensed day-care centers are as variable as the individuals who care for the babies. Some are splendid; others can be actually harmful. Knowing this, mothers recognize that choosing child care is perilous, and it is done, as a rule, with utmost caution.

Given these very practical considerations, a woman's response to leaving her baby can be as variable as the baby's response to being left by her mother. Facing, quite often, the disapproval of her family and neighbors, and finding that dependable, affectionate, and affordable child care is difficult, if not impossible, to obtain, it is no wonder that many women have difficulty leaving their children. For the woman for whom a return to outside work is neither financially nor professionally pressing, the unreliability and high cost of child care, combined with the approval she gets for being a full-time mother, can effectively postpone or prevent her leaving home.

The differences on this issue expressed by the women I interviewed were only one element of the increasing individuality of their response to the babies at this age. While, in the earlier months, several women would often give nearly identical answers to the same question, now, as the differences in the babies became more pronounced, so did the differences among their mothers. For all, what had been achieved, or what was being sought, was balance between the baby — the demands and pleasures of motherhood — and the woman's own life, the "something for myself." The solutions took many forms.

Pamela was at home, a full-time mother to her nine-month-old son and three-year-old daughter, but kept up a complicated routine, which included seeing friends regularly. She got both children into bed every night by eight, to have time to herself:

> ✌ I thought maybe with a second child I'd push him away more quickly, but I've been very involved and really haven't minded the shackling effect that it has on your life. I know it's going to be over; I know it's just a temporary thing, and that we'll get farther apart as he gets older, and as we get farther apart, there'll be more things just for me. But I've wanted to enjoy this part, and I have, though I found some of it difficult.

Her ability to envision her own future certainly contributed to Pamela's general sense of contentment:

> ✌ I think, all in all, I try to do a thoroughly good job. I work very hard at it, and I don't have much energy for anything else. I really am sort of concentrated now on being their mother, but I try to balance it with some degree of distance, so that I know that they're their own people. My involvement now comes from *my* need to be a mother. I am a mother because I want to be, and that won't be forever,

so I'm trying to think ahead. In another year I'm going to go back to school and finish my Ph.D. in art history.

Nancy, who had a son of nine months and a daughter of four years, was a physical therapist and had arranged to work just one day a week. She was certainly not working for the money, and in fact, could well have afforded to hire a sitter for the few hours a week, just to give herself some free time:

〜 I need the work for myself. I feel it helps me to be a better person when I'm with them. I go out and it's intellectually stimulating. I am confident in what I'm doing. I get a lot of feedback at work. I keep up with the field. It's a part of me that no one can touch, my own little world, and when I come home, I'm happy to see them and I'm fresh. I'm a little tired the next day, but I also get a kind of energy from my work that I don't from the children.

Rachel, who had weathered the storms and survived her misgivings about leaving Matthew, had also come to a comfortable resting point:

〜 I felt so anxious in the beginning about leaving him, and I don't anymore. Sometimes, as I walk down the steps, I see that little face looking after me, and I feel sad. I may just tell myself this to make myself feel better, but I think that having children involves a certain amount of anxiety that will continue all your life, and that to be able to deal with that anxiety is very good. As soon as you love somebody, particularly somebody who's so dependent on you, of course you're going to feel anxious. That's all right. You just have to be able to cope.

What most of the women had in common now was an ability to analyze their situations and to understand — even if they could not always achieve — what was necessary for them. Joyce, whose career as a molecular biologist was taking more of her time than she was really willing to devote to it, said:

∼ What I would really like now is a real part-time job — maybe three days a week that really took no more than four. It's the first time in my life that I've ever thought of doing that. If somebody had suggested it nine months ago, I'd have totally rejected it.

When change becomes possible, it becomes psychologically easier to accomplish it. Ellen was about to leave the job she had gone back to when Daniel was two months old for a more demanding one. The new job would require only a little more time, but much more initiative and thought on her part. I asked her why she had decided to change now:

∼ I feel there's more of my mind free of total Daniel. On a day when I'm with him all day, and then go to work at night, I'm exhausted by the time I leave the house, and then I get a second wind and wonder why I was so tired. It's an emotional tiredness; it's not purely physical, so I feel I need that kind of stimulation. It feels right to do it now. It feels like a process that's been going on since he was about six months old. Then it seemed hard. There isn't much conflict about it now. Then he was just beginning to move away, and I felt rejected, like he was moving away from me. Now I feel we're more separate, more individuals. I don't feel like he's moving away from me or me from him so much. This just has to do with me.

Alison, whose daughter was nine months old, after several false starts had completed her arrangements for returning to work. She understood why she was able to do now what had seemed so difficult three months earlier:

∼ I think, while I'm focused outward, it has to do with what I'm feeling inwardly and my place in the world, and that I have choices about that. Part of it is because the baby has changed. She'll let someone comfort her now where she wouldn't before. So I'm going back, but for completely different reasons than I would've a few months ago, like when she was five months, and I couldn't pull it off, and it seemed

187

like it was for all the wrong reasons. Now I look at it as a way to get somewhere, rather than as a way to get away from a lot of stuff.

Alison's sense that the new external order reflected a new internal balance was echoed by many others. Mother and woman were now part of a whole, and while for some, the actual time adjustments had yet to be made, there was a new recognition that integration was possible, though not always easy. For Joyce the wide difference in what was required from her in her different roles made the job of integrating her life most difficult, yet the very task of integrating was exciting:

~ The kind of energy I'm used to expending in a day is very productive and work-oriented. I produce a lot; I'm very efficient. It's like a machine. I find the time I like to spend with Zoe is totally unlike that. It's open; it has to be open time, and to go every day from being that focused on getting stuff done to being a parent in a way that really allows for exploration, for the relationship to be as spontaneous as I hope it will be, is hard. It's the hardest part for me, but it's also wonderful.

4

I asked every woman whether her relationship with her mother had changed, and every one said that it had. Every woman, without exception, hoped for approval from her mother — approval of the baby, of her mothering, of herself in general. Rachel, whose mother had died a few weeks before Rachel became pregnant with Matthew, mourned her loss and tried throughout her pregnancy and the early months of Matthew's life to find someone who might provide a mother's interest. She developed an intense and extremely unsatisfactory crush on her obstetrician, who hid behind his own professional reserve and, rather than give support during pregnancy and childbirth or approval af-

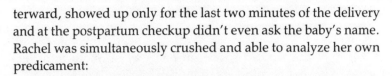

terward, showed up only for the last two minutes of the delivery and at the postpartum checkup didn't even ask the baby's name. Rachel was simultaneously crushed and able to analyze her own predicament:

> It has to do with my not having any parents. I wanted to turn him into a parent. I wanted an adult who would approve of me. I have fantasies about someone observing me and approving of what I'm doing, saying, "Oh, what a good mother."

Some grandmothers readily gave what was needed. Elaine, whose mother lived conveniently nearby, said:

> My mother's been great, really great. She comes over, and she says, "Now you just take it easy and let me fix lunch," and she's very, very supportive. We were running ourselves ragged, picking up the baby every time he made the least little sound, and she said, "You know, he'll live if you don't pick him up *every* time."

Not everyone was so lucky. Ellen described her mother, who came to stay for two weeks when Daniel was about six months old, as "very competitive. She still has to prove that she can do everything better than I can." Ellen was hurt and disappointed by her mother's attitude. Still, their relationship had improved a bit:

> I think my mother is finally starting to see me as more of an adult. There's a difference; she does treat me with more respect. I suppose that's universal.

That difference — at last becoming an adult in your own mother's eyes — did seem to be nearly universal among the women I interviewed, and they also began to look on their mothers from a new point of view. Elaine said:

> It's given me much more respect for my mother and what she went through with us. There's a bond that you

didn't have before. There's this major, major thing that you now have in common.

Many of the women spoke, in one way or another, of that sense of having been accepted into a sisterhood, of which their mothers and grandmothers were a part, whose existence they had never suspected.

Molly was my mother's first grandchild. One afternoon, when Molly was a few months old, my mother and I sat at her kitchen table, talking. I no longer recall exactly what we said, but I know that we talked of her and her mother, of me and my daughter, of mothers and daughters. I know that I had never before thought of my mother as a daughter, and I was just beginning then to think of myself as a mother. That afternoon I began to understand that I was not only Molly's mother, but *a* mother, as my mother had been and her mother before her. Motherhood, which makes us a link in the chain of generations, has, I think, for most women throughout most of history, been the one thing which has allowed us to feel a part of history, given us a hand in the making of the world, made us all a part of a great chain of being of our own.

The mother's sense of gaining a new place in *her* mother's estimation and a new place in the family is only a part of her metamorphosed sense of her self. The baby was separate, an individual, the same baby she was nine months before, yet completely different. And the mothers, the same women they were nine months before, were also completely different. Joyce, whose career had so absorbed her that she thought a child would only add to her life, but would hardly change it, said, "I feel that it's changed me all the way through."

Pamela had achieved a sense of perspective:

❧ There are a lot of things I've learned about myself. For one thing, that I really enjoy my children. Not that I didn't think I would, but in the beginning I didn't think I'd ever make it through the first year, and I've made it (or almost) and I enjoy it. I guess it's just part of the normal maturing process. Even though I feel like my life is just chaos this first year, I know that it'll be over, and I'll be able to get back to living somewhat of a normal existence again with my husband and my children. Then I'll be able to get back to school. Now I'm really confident that all these things will develop. I don't feel insecure about where I'm going in life. I feel that having the children has given me a lot of direction. Maybe it's been more settling.

This settling point at nine months is at the same time real and illusory. What is real is the achievement of an integrated self, and this will persist. Unless she has another child, this woman will not ever again sink completely into mothering as she did in the early months. Nor will she have to struggle from that immersion with the singlemindedness that was necessary at six months. The mother and the adult are there for good.

Of course, the sense of settling is also an illusion because, as the baby grows, as the mother grows, they will continue to develop and to change. The balance achieved at nine months is not stable. Ahead, and not very far, are new challenges and new contradictions that will dislodge this newly won equilibrium. For a woman, though, the knowledge and the memory of having resolved the stages of these nine months can provide the confidence she needs to surmount the challenges of her future.

Ellen, whose story began this book, has the last word:

〜 Nothing that has ever happened to me before has transformed me so completely. I'm different in every way I can think of. I don't look very different, but I have a different sense of my body, of its power. I gave birth with this body; I nourished a baby with it. I was terrified in the beginning, and I overcame my fear. I knew nothing, *nothing*, about being a mother, but I learned. I got through going back to work and changing jobs, got through what seemed like the end of my sex life forever, got through such a huge upheaval with Ed, and our marriage is still intact, and I feel

like we're better friends for what we've been through together. I look at Danny, and I'm glad that I'm the one responsible for this little boy. I walk down the street and I
see other mothers with their children, and I feel like I'm
one of them, like we all know something. I feel I've just
emerged, like a butterfly must feel coming out of the co-
coon — a metamorphosis. I look at myself in the mirror,
and I recognize myself, and I feel proud, very proud of
myself.

BACKNOTES

FOREWORD

p. 6 "We can talk of a man": Nancy Chodorow, *The Reproduction of Mothering* (Berkeley: University of California Press, 1978), p. 11.

CHAPTER 1

p. 13 "In a psychoanalytic setting": T. Berry Brazelton, "Effect of Maternal Expectations on Early Infant Behavior," *Early Child Development and Care* 2 (1973): 259–273.

p. 14 "reported by midwife Raven Lang": Marshall H. Klaus and John H. Kennell, *Maternal-Infant Bonding* (St. Louis: C. V. Mosby Co., 1976), p. 47.

p. 15 "In many other cultures": Ibid.

p. 16 "All drugs given to the mother": T. Berry Brazelton, *Doctor and Child* (New York: Delacorte, 1976), p. 30.

p. 17 "It has been postulated": N. E. Collias, "The Analysis of Socialization in Sheep and Goats," *Ecology* 37 (1956): 228.

p. 18 "A mother goat": L. Hersher, J. Richmond, and A. Moore, "Maternal Behavior in Sheep and Goats," in H. R. Rheingold (ed.), *Maternal Behavior in Mammals* (New York: John Wiley & Sons, 1963), pp. 210–211.

p. 18 "Klaus and Kennell have concluded": Klaus and Kennell, pp. 68–73.

p. 18 "a glimpse of the baby": Ibid., pp. 54–55.

p. 18 "When the baby cries": Ibid., p. 55.

p. 19 "attachment patterns": Sara S. Rode, Pi-nian Chang, Robert O. Fisch, and L. Alan Sroufe, "Attachment Patterns in Infants Separated at Birth," *Developmental Psychology* 17 (1981): 188.

p. 21 "Early separation": William Ray Arney, *Feminist Studies* 6 (1980): 560–561.

p. 21 "Infanticide": Clellan Stearns Ford, *A Comparative Study of Human Reproduction* (New Haven: Yale University Press, 1945), p. 74.

p. 22 "It is not that mothers": Klaus and Kennell, p. 52.

p. 27 "an essential principle": Ibid., p. 79.

p. 27 "estranged and unloved": Kenneth S. Robson and Howard A. Moss, "Patterns and Determinants of Maternal Attachment," *Journal of Pediatrics* 77 (1970): 976.

p. 28 "The levels of several hormones": D. A. Hamburg, R. H. Moss, and I. D. Yalom, "Distress in the Menstrual Cycle and the Postpartum Period," in R. P. Michael (ed.), *Endocrinology and Human Behavior* (London: Oxford Univeristy Press, 1968), p. 97.

p. 28 "Klaus and Kennell report": Klaus and Kennell, p. 94.

p. 28 "Proponents of home birth": Raven Lang, *The Birth Book* (Ben Lomond, Calif.: Genesis Press, 1972).

p. 30 "The mother, no matter": *Prenatal Care*, U.S. Children's Bureau (1914), p. 16.

p. 30 "Even forty years ago": Arnold Gesell and Frances L. Ilg, *Infant and Child in the Culture of Today* (New York: Harper Bros., 1943), p. 77.

p. 31 "There must be": Margaret Jarman Hagood, *Mothers of the South, Portraiture of the White Tenant Farm Woman* (Chapel Hill: University of North Carolina Press, 1939), pp. 112–113.

p. 31 "August 6, 1876": Gerda Lerner, *The Female Experience* (Indianapolis: Bobbs-Merrill, 1977), p. 77.

p. 32 "Numerous preliterate societies": Ford, op. cit., p. 67.

p. 36 "It would be good": Benjamin Spock, *Baby and Child Care* (New York: Meredith Press, 1968), p. 164.

p. 37 "As compared with neonate": John D. Benjamin, "The Innate and the Experiental in Child Development," in H. W. Brosin (ed.), *Lectures on Experimental Psychiatry* (Pittsburgh: University of Pittsburgh Press, 1961), p. 27.

p. 37 "In the first month": Richard Q. Bell, "Contributions of Human Infants to Caregiving and Social Interaction," in Michael Lewis and Leonard A. Rosenblum (eds.), *The Effect of the Infant on Its Caregiver* (New York: John Wiley & Sons, 1974), p. 5.

p. 38 "Brazelton believes": T. B. Brazelton, *Doctor and Child*, p. 45.

p. 39 "The assumption made": Elisabeth M. Magnus, "Sources of Maternal Distress in the Postpartum Period," in Jacquelynne E. Parsons (ed.), *The Psychobiology of Sex Differences and Sex Roles* (Washington, D.C.: Hemisphere Publishing Corp., 1980), p. 184.

p. 39 "But it is the woman": Ibid., p. 202.

p. 40 "Postpartum depression": Brazelton, *Doctor and Child*, p. 45.

p. 40 "One study found": R. E. Gordon, E. E. Kapostins, and K. K. Gordon, "Factors in Postpartum Emotional Adjustment," *Obstetrics & Gynecology* 25 (1965): 158.

CHAPTER 2

p. 44 "Sighted babies smile more": Selma Fraiberg, *Insights from the Blind: Comparative Studies of Blind and Sighted Infants* (New York: Basic Books, 1977), p. 98.

p. 44 "the infant becomes capable": Daniel Stern, *The First Relationship* (Cambridge, Mass.: Harvard University Press, 1977), p. 37.

p. 45 "At the age": Madelon Bedell, *The Alcotts* (New York: Clarkson N. Potter, 1980), p. 6.

p. 45 "Mothers . . . questioned": Roger Lewin, *Child Alive* (New York: Doubleday, 1975), p. 6.

p. 45 "He held a breast pad": Aiden Macfarlane, "Olfaction in the Development of Social Preferences in the Human Neonate," in M. Hofer (ed.), *Parent-Infant Interaction* (Amsterdam: Elsevier, 1975).

p. 46 "By the time smiling": John Bowlby, "The Nature of the Child's Tie to His Mother," *International Journal of Psychoanalysis* 39 (1958): 369.

p. 46 "This has been shown": R. A. Haaf and R. Q. Bell, "A Facial Dimension in Visual Discrimination by Human Infants," *Child Development* 38 (1967): 893–899.

p. 46 "Adults, too": Jacques Lacan, *The Language of the Self* (New York: Delta, 1968), p. 161.

p. 47 "moving in tune": William Condon and Louis Sander, "Synchrony Demonstrated between Movements of the Neonate and Adult Speech," *Child Development* 45 (1974): 456.

p. 47 "this synchrony becomes": T. B. Brazelton, in Klaus and Kennell, *Maternal-Infant Interaction*, p. 74.

p. 47 "love [of the baby]": Sigmund Freud, *An Outline of Psychoanalysis*, vol. 23 (Standard Edition, 1940), p. 188.

p. 47 "The infant in arms": Sigmund Freud, *Inhibitions, Symptoms, and Anxiety*, vol. 20 (Standard Edition, 1926), p. 138.

p. 48 "Were Freud in fact": H. R. Schaffer and P. E. Emerson, "The Development of Social Attachments in Infancy," *Monographs of the Society For Research in Child Development* 29 (1964a): no. 94.

p. 48 "a number of instinctual responses": Bowlby, "The Nature of the Child's Tie to His Mother," p. 365.

p. 48 "All these": John Bowlby, *Attachment* (New York: Basic Books, 1969), p. 224.

p. 49 "Institutionalized infants": Rene Spitz, "Hospitalism: An Enquiry into the Genesis of Psychiatric Conditions in Early Childhood," *Psychoanalytic Study of the Child* 1 (1945): 53–74.

p. 49 "Rhesus infants": Harry F. Harlow and M. K. Harlow, "The Affectional Systems," in A. M. Schrier, H. F. Harlow, and F. Stollwitz (eds.), *Behavior of Non-Human Primates*, vol. 2 (New York: Academic Press, 1965).

p. 50 "Ann Dally": Ann Dally, *Inventing Motherhood* (New York: Schocken, 1983).

p. 50 "Watson, a behaviorist": John B. Watson, *Psychological Care of the Infant and Child* (New York: People's Publishing Co., 1925), p. 82.

p. 51 "They would sit": Doris Lessing, *A Proper Marriage* (New York: Plume, 1964), p. 156.

p. 51 "follow your instincts": Benjamin Spock, *Baby and Child Care* (New York: Duell, Sloan and Pearce, 1957), p. 2.

p. 51 "J. S. Rosenblatt": J. S. Rosenblatt, "The Development of Maternal Responsiveness in Rats," *American Journal of Orthopsychiatry* 39 (1969): 36–56.

p. 52 "Hormones may not be": Harlow and Harlow, op. cit., p. 309.

p. 52 "Therese Benedek": Therese Benedek, "Toward the Biology of the Depressive Constellation," *Journal of the American Psychoanalytic Association* 4 (1956): 403.

p. 53 "But feeding alone": Bowlby, *Attachment*, p. 284.

p. 53 "Robson and Moss": K. S. Robson and H. A. Moss, "Patterns and Determinants of Maternal Attachment," *Journal of Pediatrics* 77 (1970): 976–985.

p. 54 "Those who have studied": K. S. Robson, "The Role of Eye-to-Eye Contact in Maternal-Infant Attachment," *Journal of Child Psychology and Psychiatry* 8 (1967): 13–25; P. H. Wolff, "Observations on the Early Development of Smiling," in B. M. Foss (ed.), *Determinants of Infant Behavior*, vol. 2 (New York: John Wiley & Sons, 1963), p. 124.

p. 54 "The pattern of sucks": P. H. Wolff, "The Role of Biological Rhythms in Early Psychological Development," *Bulletin of the Menninger Clinic* 31 (1967): 197–218.

p. 60 "Robson and Moss": Robson and Moss, op. cit., p. 980.

p. 60 "attachment *decreases*": Michael Lewis and Leonard A. Rosenblum (eds.), *The Effect of the Infant on Its Caregiver* (New York: John Wiley & Sons, 1974), p. 5.

p. 60 "All babies, of course": Silvia M. Bell and Mary D. S. Ainsworth, "Infant Crying and Maternal Responsiveness," *Child Development* 43 (1972): 1171.

p. 61 "when a baby cries": *Infant Care*, U.S. Children's Bureau (1914), p. 11.

p. 62 "What is the cry": L. Emmett Holt, *The Care and Feeding of Children*, 8th ed. (New York: D. Appleton & Co., 1916), p. 167.

p. 62 "Babies do not cry": Dorothy V. Whipple, *Our American Babies* (New York: M. Barrows, 1944), p. 86.

p. 62 "When he cries": Spock, op. cit. (1946 ed.), p. 6.

p. 63 "If a baby": Spock, op. cit. (1957 ed.), p. 175.

p. 63 "You certainly should": Lee Salk, *What Every Child Would Like His Parents to Know* (New York: Warner, 1973), pp. 21–23.

p. 63 "Klaus and Kennell": Klaus and Kennell, op. cit., p. 54.

p. 64 "have well-developed channels": Bell and Ainsworth, op. cit., p. 1185.

p. 64 "Colic has frequently": Rene Spitz, "The Effect of Personality Disturbances in the Mother on the Well-being of Her Infant," in

E. J. Anthony and Therese Benedek (eds.), *Parenthood: Its Psychology and Psychopathology* (Boston: Little, Brown, 1970), p. 507.

p. 64 "but no study has ever": Lennane and Lennane, *New England Journal of Medicine* (Feb. 1973): 290.

p. 70 "Elaine and Anne": Robson and Moss, op. cit., p. 980.

p. 71 "Separation from the baby": Rudolph Schaffer, *Mothering* (Cambridge, Mass.: Harvard University Press, 1977), p. 88.

p. 72 "Even when the mother": Schaffer and Emerson, op cit.

CHAPTER 3

p. 76 "Symbiosis describes": Margaret Mahler, Anni Bergman, and Fred Pine, *The Psychological Birth of the Human Infant* (New York: Basic Books, 1977), p. 44.

p. 78 "The anthropologists": I. DeVore and M. J. Konner, "Infancy in Hunter-Gatherer Life: An Ethological Perspective," in Norman F. White (ed.), *Ethology and Psychiatry* (Toronto: University of Toronto Press, 1974), p. 130.

p. 79 "When asleep": Louis Sander, "Infant and Caretaking Environment," in E. J. Anthony (ed.), *Explorations in Child Psychiatry* (New York: Plenum, 1975), p. 137.

p. 80 "The infant's memory": E. Aronson and S. Rosenbloom, "Space Perception in Early Infancy," *Science* 171 (1971): 1161–1163.

p. 80 "Thus if, as was done": Ibid.

p. 80 "The infant can track": Daniel Stern, *The First Relationship* (Cambridge, Mass.: Harvard University Press, 1977), p.38.

p. 81 "Human intelligence": Colwyn Trevarthen, "Early Attempts at Speech," in Roger Lewin (ed.), *Child Alive* (New York: Doubleday, 1975), p. 65.

p. 81 "It's as if": Adrienne Rich, *Of Woman Born* (New York: Norton, 1976), p. 18.

p. 82 "Margaret Mahler and her coworkers": Margaret Mahler, Fred Pine, and Anni Bergman, "The Mother's Reaction to Her Toddler's Drive for Individuation," in E. J. Anthony and Therese Benedek (eds.), op. cit., p. 260.

p. 83 "As Benedek has": Therese Benedek, "Parenthood as a Developmental Phase," *Journal of the American Psychoanalytic Association* 7 (1959): 397.

p. 84 "And if the mother's": Ibid.

p. 90 "It was after World War II": Dally, op. cit., chapter 5.

p. 90 "What is believed": John Bowlby, "Maternal Care and Mental Health," *Bulletin of the World Health Organization* 3 (1951): 366.

p. 91 "The provision": Ibid., p. 422.

p. 92 "Dally points out": Dally, op. cit., p. 6.

p. 92 "is unpredictable": Margaret Mahler, "On Human Symbiosis and the Vicissitudes of Individuation," *Journal of the American Psychoanalytic Association* 15 (1967): 750.

p. 92 "rupture of human ties": Selma Fraiberg, *Every Child's Birthright* (New York: Basic Books, 1977), p. 51.

p. 93 "The fact is": Rudolph Schaffer, *Mothering*, p. 105.

p. 93 "Studies in the United States": Urie Bronfenbrenner, "Research on the Effects of Day Care on Child Development," in *Toward a National Policy for Children and Families*, National Academy of Sciences Advisory Committee on Child Development (Washington, D.C., 1976).

p. 93 "Jerome Kagan": Jerome Kagan, "The Child in the Family," in Alice S. Rossi, Jerome Kagan, and Tamara K. Hareven (eds.), *The Family* (New York: Norton, 1978), p. 36.

p. 99 "A recent study": Richard H. Passman and Raymond K. Mulhern, Jr., *Human Behavior* (July 1978), p. 11.

p. 100 "The first and more positive": R. Q. Bell, "Contributions of Human Infants to Caregiving and Social Interaction," in Lewis and Rosenblum (eds.), op. cit., p. 9.

p. 100 "The second mechanism": Anna Freud, *The Ego and the Mechanism* (New York: International Universities Press, 1966), p. 56.

CHAPTER 4

p. 105 "The infant has": Mahler, Pine, and Bergman, op. cit., p. 58.

p. 113 "The Freudian theorists": Helene Deutsch, *The Psychology of Women* (New York: Grune and Stratton, 1944), chapter 5; Marie Bonaparte, *Female Sexuality* (New York: International Unversities Press, 1953), pp. 162–165.

p. 113 "This sorry conclusion": Nancy Friday, *My Mother, Myself* (New York: Delacorte, 1977), p. 5.

p. 113 "Adrienne Rich": Adrienne Rich, op. cit., p. 179.

p. 114 "Sexuality, the kind": This is not an original observation, but I was reminded of it while reading Ellen Willis's brilliant article, "Next Year in Jerusalem," in *Beginning to See the Light* (New York: Knopf, 1981).

p. 114 "which Erik Erikson": Erik Erikson, "Ego Development and Historical Change," *Psychoanalytic Study of the Child* 2 (1946): 363.

p. 116 "Erik Erikson defines": Ibid.

p. 118 "Erikson defines": Ibid.

p. 119 "David DeLevita lists": David DeLevita, *The Concept of Identity* (Paris: Mouton, 1965), pp. 130–131.

p. 119 ". . . both patient and therapist": H. Searles, "Anxiety Concerning Change, as Seen in the Psychotherapy of Schizophrenic Patients — with Particular Reference to the Sense of Identity," *International Journal of Psychoanalysis* 42 (1961): 81.

p. 119 "self-identity . . . emerges": Erik Erikson, *Childhood and Society* (New York: Norton, 1964), p. 211.

CHAPTER 5

p. 123 "The second accompanies": T. B. Brazelton, *Infants and Mothers* (New York: Delacorte, 1969), p. 213.

p. 123 "Since the major": Nutrition Committee of the Canadian Pediatric Society and the Committee on Nutrition of the American Academy of Pediatrics, "Breast-Feeding," *Pediatrics* 62 (1978): 591–601.

p. 124 "She is also fascinated": Michael Lewis and Jeanne Brooks-Gunn, *Social Cognition and the Acquisition of Self* (New York: Plenum Press, 1979), chapter 2.

p. 125 "there can be no": Erik Erikson, "Dr. Borg's Life Cycle," in *Adulthood* (New York: Norton, 1977), p. 12.

p. 125 "the baby has a memory": Frank Caplan, *The First 12 Months of Life* (New York: Bantam, 1978), p. 127.

p. 125 ". . . the child's relation": John Bowlby, *Maternal Care and Mental Health* (New York, Schocken, 1952), p. 13.

p. 126 "Harry Harlow": Stephen J. Suomi and Harry F. Harlow, "The Role and Reason of Peer Relationships in Rhesus Monkeys," in M. Lewis and L. A. Rosenblum (eds.), *Friendship and Peer Relations* (New York: John Wiley & Sons, 1975), p. 164.

p. 127 "The idea that the mother": Lewis and Rosenblum, *Friendship and Peer Relations*, p. 8.

p. 128 "Many babies are obviously": Schaffer and Emerson, op. cit.

p. 129 "A series of experiments": Michael Lewis and Jeanne Brooks, "Infants' Reactions to People," in M. Lewis and L. Rosenblum (eds.), *Origins of Fear* (New York: Wiley, 1974), p. 211.

p. 135 "A 1971 study": Freda Rebelsky and Cheryl Hanks, *Child Development* 42 (1971): 63.

p. 139 "The team that first": J. S. Rosenblatt, *American Journal of Orthopsychiatry* 39 (1969): 36–56.

p. 140 "Brazelton and other": Michael E. Lamb, "Father-Infant and Mother-Infant Interaction in the First Year of Life," *Child Development* 48 (1977): 167–181.

p. 141 "One researcher found": R. Parke, "Father-Infant Interaction," in M. Klaus et al. (eds.), *Maternal Attachment and Mothering Disorders, A Round Table* (Sausalito, Calif.: Johnson & Johnson, 1974).

p. 150 "One interview study": Rubin (1967), cited in Sherman, *Psychology of Women*, p. 224.

p. 153 "Carol Gilligan": Carol Gilligan, *In a Different Voice* (Cambridge, Mass.: Harvard University Press, 1982), p. 17.

p. 154 "There are deeper reasons": Nancy Chodorow, op. cit.; Dorothy Dinnerstein, *The Mermaid and the Minotaur* (New York: Harper and Row, 1977).

p. 159 "The primary argument": D. W. Winnicott, *The Child and the Family* (London: Tavistock Publications, 1957), p. 109.

CHAPTER 6

p. 161 "refueling": Margaret Mahler et al., *Psychological Birth of the Human Infant*, p. 69.

p. 162 "It is believed to affect": Jean Piaget, *On the Development of Memory and Identity* (Worcester, Mass.: Clark University Press, 1968), p. 20.

p. 164 "There is no apparent": Bettye M. Caldwell, "The Effects of Infant Care," in M. L. and L. W. Hoffman (eds.), *Review of Child Development Research*, vol. 1 (New York: Russell Sage Foundation, 1964), pp. 26–27.

p. 164 "Nursing only three or four": Committee on Drugs, American Academy of Pediatrics, Breast-Feeding and Contraception, *Pediatrics* 68 (1981): 138.

p. 167 "Differences among babies": Caplan, op. cit., p. 171.

p. 171 "Most teenagers": Sol Gordon, *The Sexual Adolescent* (Belmont, Calif.: Wadsworth, 1973), pp.37–39.

p. 171 "Those who choose": *New York Times*, August 13, 1984, p. 1.

p. 175 "Margaret Mahler theorizes": Mahler et al., op. cit., p. 60.

p. 175 ". . . the self-sacrificing mother": Sylvia Brody, "A Mother Is Being Beaten," in E. J. Anthony and T. Benedek (eds.), *Parenthood: Its Psychology and Psychopathology* (Boston: Little, Brown, 1970), p. 442.

p. 176 "resume a normal relationship": Mary Ann Cahill, *Breastfeeding and Working?* (Franklin Park, Ill.: La Leche League International, 1976), p. 24.

p. 176 "They suggest that": Ibid., pp. 8–9.

p. 179 "But the age": K. H. Tennes and E. E. Lampl, "Strangers and Separation Anxiety," *Journal of Nervous and Mental Disorders* 139 (1964): 247–254.

p. 179 "approach abruptly": Ibid.

p. 179 "keep a straight face": Rene Spitz and K. A. Wolf, "The Smiling Response: A Contribution to the Ontogenesis of Social Relations," *Genetic Psychology Monographs* 34 (1946): 57–125.

p. 179 "proceed to undress": Benjamin Spock, *Baby and Child Care* (New York: Pocket Books, 1968), p. 234.

p. 179 "In general, the experiments": G. A. Morgan and H. N. Ricciuti, in B. M. Foss, (ed.), *Determinants of Infant Behavior*, vol. 4, p. 272.

p. 179 "One investigator reports": P. H. Wolff, B. M. Foss (ed.), in *Determinants of Infant Behavior* vol. 4. (London: Methuen, 1969), p. 273.

p. 179 "Rene Spitz": Rene Spitz, *The First Year of Life* (New York: International Universities Press, 1965), p. 150.

p. 180 "It has, in fact": L. J. Cohen and J. J. Campos, "Father, Mother and Stranger as Elicitors of Attachment Behaviors in Infancy," *Developmental Psychology* 10 (1974): 146–154.

p. 181 "But as recent statistics": U.S. Bureau of the Census, *Statistical Abstract of the U.S.* (Washington, D.C.: U.S. Government Printing Office, 1984).

p. 181 "In Sylvia Brody's": Sylvia Brody, *Patterns of Mothering* (New York: International Universities Press, 1956), p. 352.

p. 181 "A study published": S. Yudkin and A. Holme, *Working Mothers and Their Children* (London: Michael Joseph, 1963).

p. 181 "In Margaret Mahler's study": Mahler, Fine, and Bergman, op. cit., p. 30.

INDEX